NEW ENGLAND
FARM
VACATIONS

A GUIDE BOOK FROM COUNTRY ROADS PRESS

LISA ANGOWSKI ROGAK

NEW ENGLAND
FARM
VACATIONS

Illustrated by
Dale Ingrid Swensson

Country Roads Press
CASTINE • MAINE

New England Farm Vacations

© 1994 by Lisa Angowski Rogak. All rights reserved.

Published by Country Roads Press
P.O. Box 286, Lower Main Street
Castine, Maine 04421

Text and cover design by Dale Ingrid Swensson.
Illustrations by Dale Ingrid Swensson.
Library of Congress Catalog Card No. 93-37245
ISBN 1-56626-044-2

Printed in the United States of America.
10 9 8 7 6 5 4 3 2 1

Library of Congress Cataloging-in-Publication Data

Rogak, Lisa Angowski.
    New England farm vacations / Lisa Angowski Rogak : illustrator,
Dale Ingrid Swensson.
        p. cm.
    ISBN 1-56626-044-2 : $9.95
    1. Hotels—New England—Guidebooks. 2. Farms—Recreational use—
New England—Guidebooks. 3. New England—Guidebooks. I. Title.
TX907.3.N35R64 1994
647.947403—dc20   93-37245
                                                        CIP

For Dan,
with much love

TABLE OF CONTENTS

Introduction   *ix*

CONNECTICUT
Barnes Hill Farm Bed & Breakfast, Sherman   3
Butternut Farm, Glastonbury   5

MAINE
Board Landing Farm, Belfast   11
Breezemere, Brooksville   13
Country Farm, Saco   15
Green Hill Farm, Ashville   17
Hamstead Farm, Bangor   20
Home Nest Farm, Kents Hill   22
Maple Hill Farm, Hallowell   24
Mari's Bed & Breakfast, Cumberland   26
Pleasant Bay Bed & Breakfast, Addison   28
Seal Cove Farm, Mount Desert   31
Snow Drift Farm, Washington   33
Squire Tarbox Inn, Wiscasset   35
Sunset House, Gouldsboro   38
Tatnic Bed & Breakfast, South Berwick   40
Welchville Inn, Oxford   43

MASSACHUSETTS
Canterbury Farm, Becket   47
Cumworth Farm, Cummington   49
Penfrydd Farm Bed & Breakfast, Colrain   51
Steep Acres Farm, Williamstown   54

NEW HAMPSHIRE

Darby Brook Farm, Alstead 59
Ellis River House, Jackson 61
Honey Lane Farm, Dublin 63
The Inn at East Hill Farm, Troy 65
Nestlenook Farm, Jackson Village 68
Peep Willow Farm, Marlborough 70
Rockhouse Mountain Farm, Eaton Center 73
Wild Goose Farm, Northwood 76
Windyledge Bed & Breakfast, Hopkinton 78

VERMONT

Broadview Farm Bed & Breakfast, St. Johnsbury 83
Harvey's Mountain View Inn & Farm, Rochester 85
Hill Farm Inn, Arlington 88
Hivue Bed & Breakfast, Brandon 90
Homeplace, Jericho 93
Hound's Folly, Mount Holly 96
Knoll Farm Country Inn, Waitsfield 98
Lake Ledge Farm, Orwell 101
Lareau Farm Country Inn, Waitsfield 104
Liberty Hill Farm, Rochester 106
Maple Crest Farm Bed & Breakfast, Cuttingsville 108
Mountain View Creamery, East Burke 110
Rose Apple Acres Farm, North Troy 112
The Inn at Shelburne Farms, Shelburne 115
West Mountain Inn, Arlington 117

INTRODUCTION

I've watched as a goat was milked by machine and as it plowed into a trough of grain while the air filled with the tanginess of fresh goat milk. I've waved away bees that were jealously guarding their hives. I've stepped into countless manure piles. In other words, I spent the summer of 1993 visiting New England farms that welcome overnight guests. As large-scale farms become the exception and small specialty farms—once called gentleman's farms—proliferate, the definition of farm has become broad.

Remember when Michael Dukakis, in his ill-fated presidential campaign, recommended specialty crops such as arugula as the solution to the country's agricultural woes? Turns out that he wasn't too far off the mark. Leave the iceberg lettuce and wheat to the megafarms in the Midwest; most of the farms in New England that are thriving are producing goat cheese, organic vegetables, and even hand-spun and -dyed llama wool.

Whether sheep farmers or tree farmers, the people who love the land also love to share their experiences with guests. In many cases, what began as a way to make a few empty rooms help pay the bills turned into a chance to educate travelers about the changing face of agriculture.

At many farms, that education comes through participation. The chores vary; depending upon the individual farm, they can range from feeding and brushing the animals to helping out during haying season.

Each farm is different—one that appeals to a family of four might hold no interest for an urban professional couple. But this individuality is the beauty of the farms. At most, since you're sleeping

in the same house as the farmer, you're bound to notice that their personality shows up everywhere in their surroundings.

The men and women who served as my farm hosts as I researched this book offered just what they promised: a bed and a meal in the morning. Many, however, went far beyond what was necessary: one host gave me free rein in his kitchen after I had arrived late one night without dinner. Another prepared a late-night snack of tea and cake for me and brought it to my room on a tray.

My sleep on a farm was always more peaceful than at home. City dwellers might find that it takes a few nights to get used to the quiet of a farm, or in some cases the sounds of cows, chickens, pigs, horses, and assorted other animals.

All the farms listed here are working farms; hence, some states have more listings than others. Of the forty-four farms in this book, I visited every one and spent the night at all but three. All include breakfast, unless otherwise noted, and some offer lunch and/or dinner as well. Most are nonsmoking; many welcome families, though some are more suited to children than others. Many are open year-round, although summer is the best time of year to visit for an authentic farm experience.

NEW ENGLAND
FARM
VACATIONS

A GUIDE BOOK FROM COUNTRY ROADS PRESS

Legend

$ = under $50 for two people, double occupancy, breakfast included
$$ = between $50 and $100
$$$ = $100 and up

B&B = bed & breakfast
MAP = Modified American Plan: breakfast and dinner
AP = American Plan: breakfast, lunch, and dinner

CONNECTICUT

Barnes Hill Farm Bed & Breakfast
Sherman

Butternut Farm
Glastonbury

Barnes Hill Farm Bed & Breakfast

Tucked away in western Connecticut, which travelers usually pass through on their way to somewhere else, is Barnes Hill Farm, a comfortable farmhouse with five guest rooms. Although its agricultural days are over, the farm still conjures up memories. It's a distance from the interstate, and its seclusion is welcome. Traffic is not a problem, even in summer.

"There's not a right angle in the house, which we love," says Sallee Johnson, who runs the bed and breakfast with her husband, Richard. The house was built in 1835 and has a total of thirty rooms, eleven of them bedrooms. The Johnsons are only the third owners since 1835; in 1987 they moved up to Sallee's native Connecticut from New Jersey, where she ran a catering service. She says that she's wanted to run a B&B ever since she was married. Today, many of the guests who come for a weekend are from New Jersey and New York City, which is only ninety minutes away.

The Johnsons spent a full year renovating the house. Their aim was to keep the home as true to its origins as possible, since it served as a guesthouse throughout the nineteenth century. Sallee tells of steaming four or five layers of wallpaper from the walls, with a coat of paint between each layer. Today, the interior of the house—especially the dining room—looks as though it's been that way since the house was built.

Sallee prepares hearty breakfasts, drawing on her catering days. Chocolate chip muffins and French toast with a hint of orange are among her menu items. Spiegel, the Johnsons' spotted beagle, might wander in for a whiff; Tweedle Dee, the cat—there once was a Tweedle Dum—will probably steer clear, preferring to get his breakfast from one of the barns that are still standing near the house. Though Barnes Hill Farm was a tobacco farm at one time, today the main crop on the five-and-a-half-acre plot is hay, which the farmer across the road cuts in summer. In winter, he takes guests for sleigh rides in horse-drawn sleighs.

Also across the road is a pick-your-own raspberry farm that guests like to frequent. Sallee tends a vegetable garden, where she grows the herbs that she cooks with at breakfast. The land that surrounds the farm is owned by a local land trust, which ensures that the property will be kept open and undeveloped.

The guest rooms all have private baths, queen-sized beds, and antique furnishings. Outdoors, there's a Jacuzzi on the deck, rosebushes, a picnic table, and fields of wildflowers.

Once a year in summer, the Johnsons have a huge barbecue and hoedown at the farm for their annual church supper, and guests staying that night are welcome to join in.

Sallee and Richard Johnson
Barnes Hill Farm Bed & Breakfast
29 Route 37 East
Sherman, CT 06784
203-354-4404
$$
Children welcome
Open year-round

Butternut Farm

Five miles outside of Hartford is a place you would never believe existed. There is so much to see—and so much that reveals itself only the third and fourth time you've walked through this circa 1720 house—that one night at Butternut Farm is simply not enough.

Don Reid has been running the bed and breakfast at Butternut Farm for more than seventeen years. The four guest rooms have period furnishings from eighteenth-century Connecticut, and the rest of the large classic Colonial follows suit. Except for some modern amenities, the old house is as intact as it can be, with wide plank floors made from pumpkin pine, a wide front door, and a massive hearth in the dining room. From the old clocks and framed maps and samplers that hang on the walls to the tin wall sconces that still hold candles, you have to spend ten minutes in each room just taking everything in. And even then you're bound to miss some things. The bedrooms feature antique pencil-post beds with lace canopies. There are chocolates and sherry in every guest room.

The common rooms adjoin each other: first a parlor, then a sitting room, then another more formal room that looks like an eighteenth-century office. In the yard is a 1700s barn where Don plays classical music for the animals, which include—on a mere two acres—ten Swiss Alpine milking goats, bantam chickens, prizewinning white-tailed pigeons, doves, and a goose named Harry. Geese are relentless property guards, and Harry is no exception. He'll head straight for your shoes, his long neck low to the ground, indignant honks coming from his beak as he rushes toward you. I fought him off with a legal pad with a thick cardboard back. Don assuages the bird by saying, "Oh, Harry, that's quite enough," and the goose stops. Sometimes Don slips and calls him Harriet, which is understandable—after a few months of calling him Harry, one morning he found "him" sitting on some eggs. So now, either name works.

In addition to the guest rooms in the house, there is an apartment in the barn. The walls are a foot thick, so if you want to hear farm sounds,

Harry—or Harriet—the "watchdog" goose

you must open the windows. Although the house is on Glastonbury's main street, you won't hear traffic sounds, owing to the high picket fence around the property. In fact, there's no sign for the farm, so be sure to follow Don's directions exactly.

In the yard is an immaculate garden complete with a stone-lined path, statues, and a small carp pool. A wildflower garden contains a fountain, stone walks, and a table and chairs.

Don has worked as a banker, then as a teacher in the thirty-two years that he's lived in the house. He got into the B&B business when a woman up the street who had a B&B had no vacancies one evening and asked Don if he'd take some guests.

He says he frequently drops hints to guests about helping out with chores, but "they don't always pick up on it." He does enjoy taking guests through the house, walking you through a bit impassively, but secretly gleeful when he sees, out of the corner of his eye, your mouth drop open at the sights.

For breakfast, Don serves fresh fruit, freshly squeezed orange juice, eggs scrambled with cheese and herbs, and home-baked sourdough corn bread. He good-naturedly encourages guests: "You're going to eat more than that, aren't you?"

Don Reid
Butternut Farm
1654 Main Street
Glastonbury, CT 06033
203-633-7197
$$
Children welcome
Open year-round

MAINE

Board Landing Farm
Belfast

Breezemere
Brooksville

Country Farm
Saco

Green Hill Farm
Ashville

Hamstead Farm
Bangor

Home Nest Farm
Kents Hill

Maple Hill Farm
Hallowell

Mari's Bed & Breakfast
Cumberland

Pleasant Bay Bed & Breakfast
Addison

Seal Cove Farm
Mount Desert

Snow Drift Farm
Washington

Squire Tarbox Inn
Wiscasset

Sunset House
Gouldsboro

Tatnic Bed & Breakfast
South Berwick

Welchville Inn
Oxford

Board Landing Farm

"I have my own little universe here," says Andree Lawrence of Board Landing Farm. "There's no other place I'd want to be."

Indeed, the house, built in the 1890s high on a ledge overlooking the Passagassawakeag River, is just the type of place that a city person loves to escape to. The house has high ceilings, lots of books, a light airy kitchen, and a hostess who leaves the farm only reluctantly because everything she needs is here.

Board Landing has only one guest room, so you're bound to feel spoiled. The farm was named because down at the river, reached via a wide, grassy path, a sawmill once stood; part of the foundation still stands. The house seems tucked away deep in the country, yet it's only a five-minute drive from the center of busy Belfast. The Lawrences take out guests in a motorboat, and also invite them to participate in activities if they're doing something they think the guests would like.

Andree runs the eighty-acre, seventy-five-goat farm with the help of her husband, Deane, and her children, Aaron, who's ten, and her four-year-old daughter, Skye. Guests are welcome to help out with the animals and chores if they wish. Andree raises goats and one llama for fleece; a few chickens and geese wander around. Andree is usually accompanied by Shadow, the farm's everpresent black Lab, or by some of the barn cats. She raises a type of goat known as cashgora, a combination of cashmere and angora goat. She sells their fleece and felts, which are like sheepskin rugs without the skin, and is happy to show guests how to make a felt from fleece.

The Lawrences are vegetarian, and serve a macrobiotic breakfast, in addition to the more standard fare of eggs, toast, and yogurt. They also make their own honey. The area between the kitchen and the dining room is open so that guests can chat with Andree while she's making breakfast. People get so comfortable at Board Landing, says Andree, that many relax in the house until noon, a rarity at many B&Bs.

After all, in the backyard there's a fenced-in play area with a wooden swing. Children can play while parents watch through the French doors and linger over another cup of coffee in the dining room. Aaron and Skye love to play with guests' children. The one guest bedroom with the pullout couch can easily fit a family of four.

Guests can look at the animals, go fishing and swimming in the river, help fill water buckets, or boat into Belfast in the same time it takes to drive. Board Landing is open year-round. In winter, Deane, a landscape architect by trade, clears cross-country ski trails in the farm's pastures and forest.

It's unusual to find a bed and breakfast with only one guest room, but Andree likes it that way; she says that it seems less like a business and more like an opportunity to share their lives on the farm. The one room has a queen-sized bed looking out onto the garden, and a bathroom that used to be a bedroom, which explains its size. A clawfoot tub sits on a platform two steps up, and there's a shower around the corner. A high double sink with antique light fixtures above it fills an entire wall.

Andree and Deane Lawrence
Board Landing Farm
RFD 2, Box 120
Belfast, ME 04915
207-338-2325
$$
Children welcome
Open year-round

Breezemere

Upon my arrival at Breezemere on Penobscot Bay, I pulled into the parking lot next to the main house and was immediately shushed by a man and woman sitting in the next car. They were staring into a field watching a fox stalk a fawn. The man and woman—Linda Forest, who owns Breezemere with her husband, Joe, and their friend Jim Gibson, who occasionally fills in at the inn—told me they had been watching this intricate dance for twenty minutes.

So I watched, too. The fox would start to close in on the fawn, who seemed to view the motion as a game. The fawn would then back away, which would startle the fox, who then seemed even more intent on backing the fawn against the stone wall.

This continued for at least another twenty minutes. Suddenly, the fox ran off into the woods, and the fawn looked a bit confused at having its game interrupted.

That's the kind of wildlife you'll find at Breezemere. Joe and Linda have been running the place, which is open from May through October, for four years now. They spend winters in Sonoma County, California. Before they bought the twenty-seven-acre resort on the Blue Hill peninsula, the Forests owned a commercial vineyard where they raised grapes to sell to wineries. Joe's family had summered in this part of Maine since the 1880s, and when the inn came up for sale, they bought it.

The Forests have tried their luck at a number of different farm animals over the years, including pigs, sheep, and rabbits, but the seasonality of the inn made it hard to find local people to take the animals in winter. They also had ducks, but the fox had better luck with them than it had with the fawn. The Forests decided not to replace the animals, though they still do some haying.

Linda keeps an organic garden, which guests are invited to help out with in between exploring the trails behind the main farmhouse and sitting in one of the Adirondack chairs in front of Breezemere's lodge.

The Blue Hill peninsula's rolling hills lure bicyclists who like a bit of a challenge. The small hills that make up most of Brooksville's main roads remind me of skiing moguls, except they're more spread out.

Guests can stay in one of the seven rustic cottages scattered over the hill behind the main farmhouse—with a commanding view of the fox pasture—or in the cottages down by the bay. The Hawthorne honeymoon cottage sits at the end of the hilly trail and contains two bedrooms, a bath with a clawfoot tub, a small sitting area, a kitchen, and a fireplace.

In the farmhouse, which was built in 1850, there are seven bed-and-breakfast rooms, all named after places in Maine. I stayed in the Monhegan, a spacious room on the third floor with a private bath and a wonderful view of the bay. Breakfast is served on the screened porch of the lodge across the road, which reminded me of a summer camp rainy-day building, all wood and high ceilings, and the requisite out-of-tune upright piano.

The meals at Breezemere are nothing like camp food, however. Blueberry pancakes and homemade muffins are breakfast staples. Dinner, available Monday through Thursday in July and August, features organic produce from Linda's garden. No matter the time of day, gull cries permeate the air, so sit out front in one of the chairs and watch them fly.

Linda and Joe Forest
Breezemere
Brooksville, ME 04617
207-326-8628 or 800-637-0794
$$, dinner optional
Children welcome
Open May through October

Country Farm

The cow trinkets scattered around Arlene and Norman Gonneville's farmhouse at Country Farm attest to the main occupation here. Though Norman gave up milking seven years ago, an unfortunate yet common side effect of dairy farming in New England—five years ago there were twelve dairy farms in the neighborhood, now there are only two—Norman still has one foot in the business, selling milk for a large local dairy. But when he and Arlene gave up the farm, they started the bed and breakfast, so their loss was really a gain for guests, at least.

There are still thirty-five beef cattle in the pasture that has frontage on the Saco River, along with a couple of old dairy trucks with the words "Gonneville Dairy" painted on them. In fact, if you stay in the back bedroom at Country Farm, there's a good chance you'll wake up to the sound of cows (and a horse) munching on grass by the back of the house.

At many of New England's smaller farm B&Bs, the main attraction is not the livestock but the cats, and Country Farm is no exception. Instead of barn cats whose main function is mousing, the cats at Country Farm mostly reside on the porch. When I visited, there were no less than six cats, including an unusual seventeen-year-old scrawny black cat named Minnie who has no voice. Arlene's cousin Louise, who helps out at the farm occasionally, says it's the smallest collection of cats they've had in a long time.

Even though Saco is right in the middle of prime Maine oceanfront country, there are plenty of visitors who prefer a farm to the ocean. "We get people all the time who call us up when we're full, and I'll say 'Try the beach,' but they don't want the beach," says Arlene. "They want a farm."

Behind the house is an immense hayfield, where children enjoy romping. In the middle of the hayfield is a small fenced-in cemetery with toppled stones that Arlene wants to restore. Down on the river, there's a small beach with a campfire area tucked away on the shore. Guests can rent inner tubes and canoes nearby, or just go swimming. On the porch with the cats is an old-fashioned, squeaky floor swing glider, although the noise is nothing compared to the racket that Mike, the resident ghost, makes when he walks around upstairs. Ask Arlene about Mike the Ghost, who drowned in 1932 getting water from the Saco River, and who still hangs around to see that everything is done to his liking.

Mike the Ghost is silent during breakfast, showing his approval. Breakfast at Country Farm is twice what I would ever eat, but somehow I managed to try everything. Arlene's daughter, Michelle, lives across the street and cooks breakfast when her mother's not around, and she doesn't hesitate to pull out all the stops. Omelets, cereal, homemade muffins, fruit, juice, potatoes, and a fancy bread with ham and cheese tucked inside all filled the table. But Arlene will accommodate anyone, remembering the time that one guest wanted plain cauliflower, broccoli, and carrots for breakfast. Arlene provided it.

Try to visit Country Farm on Columbus Day weekend, when the farm holds its annual scarecrow contest. One year, a girl dressed as a scarecrow and entered the contest. Everything was fine until a judge stuck a number on her and she started to move.

Arlene and Norman Gonneville
Country Farm
139 Louden Road
Saco, ME 04072
207-282-0208
$$
Children welcome
Open year-round

Green Hill Farm

At thirty-five-acre Green Hill Farm, only forty-five minutes from Bar Harbor, you'll find angora rabbits, five sheep named Veronica, Princess, Spike, Sue, and Shy, a vegetable garden, and an apple orchard featuring old varietals that make good cider and apple butter. The farm's size is plenty for Nuna Cass, but not for her husband, Ted, who grew up in Iowa on what, he says, "constitutes a farm."

Nuna disagrees, along with many other gentlemen and -women farmers in New England who keep a small garden and even smaller herd of livestock. After all, before the Casses moved to Maine in 1985, they lived in Iowa, and Nuna kept a flock of six sheep there.

But no matter. Nuna is a good farmer and Ted is a self-described good talker, especially when May comes, after there have been no guests since September. "You sit down at the kitchen table," says Nuna, "and whoosh! You're captured."

The couple have eclectic interests, which spark lively conversations

Sheep at Green Hill Farm

with the guests. Nuna, for example, keeps busy in winter with spinning and dying the wool from Veronica & Company, and making custom-designed sweaters. One-third of the guests are European. Nuna speaks Danish, and Ted worked as a Spanish teacher back in Iowa. When they moved to Ashville they specifically sought a house that could support a seasonal B&B, themselves, and assorted animals, though as Nuna jokes, "We started the B&B because we had too many blankets." They've been running the B&B since 1987. They are accustomed to having a variety of people living in their house, since they sheltered foreign and exchange students back in Iowa.

The Casses started the B&B without knowing they were carrying on a longtime tradition on the farm. The original Route 1 ran right past the house, and Green Hill had previously served as a popular tourist home in the 1920s and 1930s. In fact, Nuna found an old sign in the attic that advertised rooms and meals in the farmhouse. Built in 1820, the house remained in the same family until the Casses bought it.

Nuna likes to do the chores before guests get up, though she encourages guests to help put hay in the feeder and carry water out to the sheep. Because sheep can be very skittish around strangers, she suggests that guests take a few slices of bread to make friends, and even that's no guarantee.

The sheep pen is close to the house to discourage predators, so when Nuna gets up to do the chores she has to tiptoe around in the dark; if the sheep see her walking around in the kitchen they'll start bleating and wake up everyone.

Green Hill has two bedrooms with a shared bath available for guests. One room has a three-quarter bed, a rocker, and a cottage pine dresser; the other room has two twin beds. The bedrooms are located just off a second-floor landing that is extra wide; the house used to be a center chimney cape, and what's now a staircase with a shiny banister used to accommodate a chimney.

Nuna serves a traditional country breakfast, and asks guests the night before if they want French toast, omelets, muffins, or just coffee and juice. She tells of guests who have worked their way up the Maine coast at bed and breakfasts, and by the time they reach Green Hill, all they want is toast and coffee. Nuna is happy to oblige them.

Nuna and Ted Cass
Green Hill Farm
RR 1, Box 328
Ashville, ME 04607
207-422-3273
$
Children "under crawling age and over seven welcome"
Open May through September

Hamstead Farm

Ray and Lillian Little, who run Hamstead Farm just outside of Bangor in Hermon, approached farming the opposite way from most farmers. Most New Englanders who have twenty Black Angus beef cattle, seventeen calves, six pigs, a hundred turkeys, and 150 acres of land usually have manure in their blood: their great-great-great-great-grandparents started farming the land a couple of centuries ago, and every generation since has followed their example too, usually on the same plot of land.

The Littles did it differently. Ray's father was a banker, and Lillian's was a plumber, with no farming in their backgrounds. One day, all that changed. "We started with six chickens and our daughter's 4-H project seventeen years ago, and we've been farming ever since," says Lillian.

With such a variety of animals, guests who want to help out with chores will have their hands full, mucking out pigpens, feeding animals, and weeding the vegetable garden. Once, a guest even got up in the middle of the night to help out while a calf was being born. "Some watch, some help a lot or a little, and some don't even want to look," says Lillian.

Guests who want to just relax have ample opportunity in the Littles' 1846 house, which contains a few special touches. On the staircase that leads up to the two guest rooms, family pictures hang on the wall, and Lillian did the stenciling that adorns the walls. The cradle on the landing at the top of the stairs belonged to Ray's grandmother; the long, low wooden box in the downstairs hallway is an old feedbox. Old-fashioned fire extinguishers that resemble something Rube Goldberg might have invented are found in a few of the rooms. Their milky glass globes are held high by a band of low-heat metal screwed into the door jamb. The premise behind them is that when the metal gets hot, it expands and loosens, which sends the globe hurtling to the floor. The glass breaks, and some unnamed fire retardant falls on the fire and puts it out. It also smells. One day, a couple of guest's children eyed the fire extinguishers. They disengaged a globe and proceeded to play catch with it. Of course, one missed and dropped it, sending the fumes all through the house.

But Lillian, who likes to see families stay at Hamstead, didn't even blink. In fact, when a family with three children recently visited, she let them each pick an animal they were responsible for feeding for the entire week. They loved it.

There are a few sitting areas downstairs where guests can relax. Baskets filled with magazines are in every common room and bedroom, and there's also a TV. The Littles' black Lab named Hannah is personable enough, except when she's lying on her daybed in the kitchen. Along with most farm hosts, even dogs need their private space.

Outside, you can sit on the deck or in the shade near the garden, listen to the turkeys near the old apple orchard, and witness the ways of a farm. "Check out that one," Ray said, pointing to a big tom turkey who was strutting his stuff in front of the henhouse. "He's trying to impress the girls."

"He's wasting his time," Lillian responded. "He's already sold for a barbecue next Tuesday."

Lillian and Ray Little
Hamstead Farm
RD 2, Box 703
Bangor, ME 04401
207-848-3749
$
Children welcome
Open year-round

Home Nest Farm

History is the mainstay at Home Nest, located in an area of Maine that is quite beautiful in its isolation. In fact, like many small towns in rural New England, Kents Hill boasts of an earlier time when the area was bustling with activity. But today, to look at it, you'd never know.

Except if you stayed at Home Nest, which is replete with mementos that point back to that lost time. Arn Sturtevant's family started here in the 1780s on a plot of land that was granted to the family right after the revolutionary war. Old photos of Arn's ancestors hang throughout the house, and an old bayonet rifle from the revolutionary war hangs over the fireplace in the sitting room in the main house. Over the piano is a case full of his great-grandfather's Civil War trinkets. In fact, Arn remembers sitting with Helen Ormsby Sturtevant, his great-grandmother, in the parlor as she taught him scripture from the family's illustrated, rodent-chewed Bible. To reward him for learning a few verses, she took out her husband's Civil War medals and let him play with them.

In fact, his great-grandmother always referred to the unnamed farm as Home Nest, and the name stuck when the Sturtevants opened the B&B in 1987. One room in the house has built-in Shaker drawers. The two-bedroom suite upstairs was part of the original saltbox house built in 1784. The shelves hold lots of antique bottles and glass candlesticks that Arn found in an old dump on the farm.

Arn grew up in nearby Livermore Falls, and recalls visiting Home Nest with his father in the 1940s, when the farm was vacant. He and Leda moved here in 1975.

In addition to the upstairs suite, the main building holds a four-room suite: a bedroom, two living rooms—one with a TV—and a fully equipped kitchen. Everything here is original, from the hearth to the wide-board floors. The bed is a pencil-post canopy that you have to climb up into.

While you sleep, elves are hard at work. You see, Home Nest is technically not a bed and breakfast, except for guests who stay in the upstairs suite. Early in the morning, Leda sneaks into the kitchen in the four-room apartment and sets the table, makes coffee, sets up the electric frying pan, and puts out containers of pancake batter and fresh blueberries. I wish I had the same elves living at my house.

There are twenty sheep at Home Nest, along with one horse and a pony. The Sturtevants raise the sheep for wool, and started keeping animals to keep the pastures open and the woodlands from growing back. It worked. Out back, there are blueberry bushes and a stately memorial for a family horse that died a few years ago.

In addition to the farmhouse, there's the Lilac cottage—a two-story house built in the 1790s—across the road, where guests can stay. The newest building at Home Nest is the red schoolhouse, built in 1830 and moved to the farm from one and a half miles away. It had been abandoned for twenty years when the Sturtevants bought it and fixed it up. One of their children lives there now, but in past years, guests have stayed in it.

The sense of history is so pervasive at Home Nest that Arn wrote a book about his great-grandfather, called *Josiah Volunteered*, a copy of which is found in every room in Home Nest.

Leda and Arn Sturtevant
Home Nest Farm
Box 2350
Kents Hill, ME 04349
207-897-4125
$$
Children welcome
Open year-round

Maple Hill Farm

In much of New England, if you drive a couple miles in any direction from the center of town, chances are good that you'll find yourself in rolling farmland. Drive five minutes from the middle of Augusta, the capital of Maine, and you'll find yourself at Maple Hill Farm, a casual sixty-two-acre farm where the main crops are hay and wood.

"We get a lot of New Yorkers," says Scott Cowger, who owns the farm with his partner Robert Audet. "They come and stay by themselves and eat by themselves, and then after the first few days they loosen up, relax, and mingle."

Though the cooked-to-order breakfast is a little on the fancy side—eggs Benedict and freshly ground coffee are staples at Maple Hill—Cowger and Audet welcome children. Following is a report by my ten-year-old son, Christopher Brendan, who accompanied me on my visit to the farm, which features an unusual double-gambrel–style house:

> Maple Hill Farm is a great place for children and adults. For children, there's a big screen TV with laser disc and CD players. The service is very nice. The owners, Scott and Robert, are always glad to play cards with you, or show you how the TV works, or answer any questions you have about anything. Rob and Scott's twelve-year-old cat George, who looks like Morris, is very friendly. But don't touch his tail!

Hayfields surround the house, and there's a vegetable and herb garden out back. Robert and Scott also make maple syrup in spring, and they plan to get a few workhorses to help out with the load in the next couple of years. The farm abuts a 550-acre protected nature preserve, and you can frequently see porcupines and deer. An old stone wall cuts across the back of the property, parting for a trail that cuts through the woods for walking or cross-country skiing.

Besides an inn and farm, Maple Hill also features a small conference center in the carriage house on the property, which can accommodate meetings of up to forty-five people. With the farm's proximity to Augusta, state and local legislators frequently stay at Maple Hill.

It's better than staying at a hotel if you're looking for personal touches such as a wake-up knock and your name instead of a room number in a slot on your bedroom door. And plants, fresh flowers, and antiques are in every room.

Future plans that Scott and Robert have for the inn are an art gallery that focuses on new Maine artists, and a simple cafe that serves breakfast and lunch to the public.

Scott Cowger and Robert Audet
Maple Hill Farm
RR 1, Box 1145
Hallowell, ME 04347
207-622-2708
$$
Children welcome
Open year-round

Mari's Bed & Breakfast

When you walk in the door of Mari's Bed and Breakfast, located in a quiet bedroom community of Portland, the first thing that owner Mary Lalumiere does is ask if you've eaten dinner, or if you want some cookies, or if you need to do some laundry. This kind of hospitality is evident every minute you spend at Mari's, a comfortable five-bedroom Victorian farmhouse built in 1898. Many guests return again and again, just to see Mary. It's like going back to an aunt or a grandmother's house as an adult.

There are several sitting rooms downstairs, a big front porch, and even an in-ground swimming pool in the backyard. Mary's fifteen-acre "farm" consists of marigolds, buttercups, roses, thistle, clover, daisies, and juniper that she specially cultivates in her backyard to incorporate into the more than four thousand pieces of pottery she makes in her basement every year. There are flowers around the pool, at the edge of the grass, and along the property lines. She gives guests a piece of pottery when they leave.

In addition to the B&B and her pottery business, Mary also works part-time as a nurse. Unlike many busy people, however, when she sits down to talk with you, it feels as though she has all the time in the world.

"I run the bed and breakfast like a family," she says, adding that she comes from a family of five who lived on a farm with a guesthouse that had seven rooms, so she's used to having lots of people around. She invites guests to come with her on walks to collect flowers from other places, or to come with her on her morning bike ride or swim. Guests can also watch Mary as she creates her pottery.

"In the B&B business, you have to come across that you're not afraid of people, and that most people are basically good," she says. "One time I had eleven guests and thirteen people at breakfast, and we hung around the dining room table and went through five pots of coffee by the time we were done. It was 11 A.M. when everybody left and I went back to work, but it was great, I loved every minute of it."

That effervescence was what got her into the bed-and-breakfast business in the first place. In 1987, a local realtor asked Mary if she would take in a family who was moving to the area. Their house in Illinois had sold more quickly than they had anticipated. The family of four moved in for four months. She saw it as a testing ground for the B&B and officially opened in 1988. Ever since, half of her business has been guests who have been to Mari's at least twice.

The house feels warm and cozy, even in the large rooms. A room in the front has a piano, and there's an old-fashioned parlor stove in the back living room. The sofas in the living room are the kind you can sink into, and there's a TV for anyone to watch.

If you want to be a child again, being thoroughly spoiled for a few days by your favorite aunt, spend a few days at Mari's.

Mary Lalumiere
Mari's Bed & Breakfast
POB 308
Cumberland, ME 04021
207-829-3321
$$
Children welcome
Open year-round

Pleasant Bay Bed & Breakfast

When you first drive up to the house at Pleasant Bay and pass pastures with more than a few llamas looking at you curiously, you know this is a serious llama farm. When you reach the Jeep in the driveway with the vanity plate that says HUMMM 2, you know you've arrived. Mother llamas hum to their babies, and at least a dozen baby llamas are born at Pleasant Bay each year. In fact when I visited in late summer, a two-day-old sleek black llama that was all legs was gamboling around the pasture by her mother's side.

Pleasant Bay is off Maine's beaten path—it's less than an hour to the Canadian border. You can admire the view from the deck, wander around the farm's 110 acres and four miles of trails—with a llama in tow if you choose—or just relax. Lee and Joan Yeaton built their spacious, airy house five years ago, though it feels more like an old house with the

You can be sure the llamas will check you out

obvious attention the Yeatons have paid to detail, such as old beams, and antique furnishings placed throughout the house.

The three bed-and-breakfast rooms are tastefully decorated, and all share a view of the bay. Though Joan places a chocolate on your pillow, the atmosphere is not at all stuffy. Half the guests come for the water access and half come for the llamas, though by the end of their stay each group has overlapped. There's a sandy cove where you can brave the water that's icy even in August, or you can go out in the Yeatons' canoe. Local tour companies run puffin and whale-watch trips, and nearby Addison Marsh attracts legions of bird-watchers.

Llama aficionados can spend all day in the woods with the llamas, talking to them and hiking with them. Guests can also help feed and brush them. Many people view llamas as exotic animals. Joan encourages everyone to become better acquainted with these regal, almost polite creatures. In fact, more than a few guests visit Pleasant Bay and go home with a llama. Though not all llamas are friendly, Joan compares them to cats: "If they're interested, they're all over you," she says.

In addition to the thirty llamas, Pleasant Bay has a couple of dogs and cats, a variety of kittens at any one time, and chickens that like to be petted. Guests can also pick blueberries and raspberries in season from the bushes that line the trails and dot the hills, and can poke around an old cemetery that the Yeatons uncovered when they first began to clear the land.

Joan and Lee started the B&B because they knew they'd be tied down with the farm, and they wanted a way to travel by staying home. Pleasant Bay is open year-round, with a 40 percent occupancy rate in winter and 95 percent in summer. After raising six children of their own, the Yeatons welcome children on the farm. Lee even takes children out for tractor rides over the trails and through the llama pastures.

When Joan asks you the night before what you want for breakfast the next morning, ask for her popover pancake, which is just as it sounds, and served with fresh fruit and maple syrup. She'll also serve dinner to guests for a fee if notified a day ahead. Because the B&B is in Maine, lobster, of course, is the featured attraction. But don't look for Joan to hop in the HUMMMmobile and run to the store for some live ones. Down in the bay, the lobstermen cruise by the shoreline at regular intervals, checking their pots. When Joan needs a few lobsters, she'll walk down to the bay and hold up a sign with the number of lobsters she needs. Around three in the afternoon she'll go down and pick them up.

Joan and Lee Yeaton
Pleasant Bay Bed & Breakfast
Box 222, West Side Road
Addison, ME 04606
207-483-4490
$$, dinner optional
Children welcome
Open year-round

Seal Cove Farm

Seal Cove Farm is a big, busy farm with goats, cats, and children all squealing and running around in the yard while the adults—hosts and guests alike—go about their chores, smiling at the constant antics as they go.

Seal Cove is on the quiet side of Mount Desert Island, but judging from the boisterousness of the farm, you'd never know it. No matter, Barbara Brooks keeps the bed and breakfast under control with the help of her mother, Floss, who cooks breakfast for guests in summer. Sheer numbers explain the exuberance of the farm: seventy goats, with thirty-eight that are milked twice a day; various barn cats; a dog named Katie; a pony named Twilight; chickens, turkeys, and pigs; two children—Gard is eight and his sister, Sally, is four; three comfortable guest rooms; and a garden with lettuce, corn, potatoes, raspberries, and more. And Barbara makes two hundred pounds of cheese a week from the goats' milk, and sells it to local gourmet stores and farmers' markets.

Need I go on? Seal Cove is a delight, even for people who aren't used to the bustle. "Some guests like to help out in the garden, while others just follow us around," says Barbara. "After people are here for a few days, they see that farming is not the romantic life they think it is; the hard work shows through. The closeness with the earth is what's missing in everyday life, and some guests really start to crave that."

The farmhouse is huge, with the high ceilings endemic to houses built in the second half of the nineteenth century. Built in 1875 for a sea captain, the house has served as a post office and as a boardinghouse in years past. Two of the guest rooms share a bath. White fluffy down comforters and many pillows grace the queen-sized beds in rooms that are light and airy. The two front guest rooms and the breakfast room look out onto Seal Cove Pond and Western Mountain across the way.

Since the farm is family oriented, Barbara's children interact with the guests, even at breakfast, when little Sally brings in another cinnamon roll or plate of bacon smoked from the farm's own pigs. After breakfast, you can sit on the back porch while tiny kittens bite your shoelaces and try to climb up your leg and into your lap. A few goats wander around loose. The mechanical vacuum sounds of the milking machine provide a steady rhythmic background for the other farmyard sounds—clucking, meowing, and neighing—that provide the melody.

Seal Cove is a few miles from Acadia National Park and a public boat launch. "We don't have to go outside for stimulation, since people come to us," says Barbara. But at Seal Cove, it also works the other way around.

Barbara and Floss Brooks
Seal Cove Farm
HCR 62, Box 140
Mount Desert, ME 04660
207-244-7781
$$
Children welcome
Open year-round

Snow Drift Farm

If you were to suddenly pack your urban bags and move to live year-round at Snow Drift Farm, in the town of Washington, you probably wouldn't complain, as city people do, about the lack of cultural stimulation in a rural community. You probably wouldn't even have to leave the house.

Arlene and George Van Deventer are an eclectic, well-read, and enthusiastic couple who do everything with gusto, whether it's talking with guests or renovating their circa 1861 house, which, when they bought it, had only two light bulbs and no running water.

George runs local poetry workshops and sings in statewide operatic productions. Arlene teaches first grade, plays the organ, and speaks some German. A wonderfully large, diverse collection of books lines the walls of the living room, which has a baby grand piano at one end. Alongside the VCR is the complete collection of the PBS Civil War series. One of the guest rooms has an almost-complete collection of Agatha Christie mysteries.

But it wasn't always this way. Ask to see the photos of the old house before the renovation. It bears little resemblance to the comfortable rooms that are today a haven for travelers.

When they moved up to Maine from New Jersey twenty years ago, George was a truck driver and Arlene was a teacher. "When we moved here, we wanted to do a little pottery and raise a few goats," says Arlene, laughing. "By the time we were done, we had a 120-head dairy farm and a totally renovated house."

Like many dairy farmers in New England, economics forced George to sell the cows in 1989. Today, he concentrates on haying, though he still keeps six cows, primarily for pets, he says. After the other cows were sold, George and Arlene still wanted to use the property—they own seventy-three acres—and opened the B&B the year after, though they had been thinking about it for years.

Recently, the Van Deventers put in a nature trail, which doubles as a cross-country ski trail in winter. They also encourage guests to use a swimming hole in a stream on their land. Other guests go fly-fishing or just walk down the road. George tells of a family who visited the farm and walked the paths, went fly-fishing, and cooked dinner in the kitchen. "Many people are hesitant about using the common rooms in a bed and breakfast," says George. "Our farm is meant to be used, and this family used the property the way I like to see it used."

Snow Drift also has an unusual amenity for a farm: if your body is weary from too much traveling, there's a nearby massage therapist who will come and relax you.

Frequently on farm vacations the nonfarm animals get the most attention from guests. Newton is Snow Drift Farm's resident black Lab, and has one trick. Ask George and Arlene to ask Newton to do it.

Arlene and George Van Deventer
Snow Drift Farm
RR 1, Box 669
Washington, ME 04574
207-845-2476
$
Children welcome
Open year-round

Squire Tarbox Inn

Squire Tarbox is where I fell in love with goats. No surprise there. Even though innkeepers Karen and Bill Mitman have eleven tastefully deco-rated rooms in the inn—part of which dates back to 1763—and they serve delicious gourmet dinners prepared with a particular eye toward detail, Bill perhaps put it best: "We're goatherders who rent out rooms."

Well, not quite. They've been raising goats for thirteen years since they dropped out of the corporate rat race in Boston. They began with a couple of goats at a farm they rented on Deer Isle and started making cheese because they had too much milk.

You'll fall in love with the nanny and her kids

Today, Karen makes more than three thousand pounds of hard and soft cheese each year in a two-room cheese plant downstairs. Nothing goes to waste: she also makes yogurt and feta cheese for the inn, and uses the leftover whey in breads and pastries.

The inn is on quiet Westport Island, only a short drive from Wiscasset or Bath. The Mitmans say that staying at the inn is like having a French countryside experience on the Maine coast, which is a pretty accurate description. It's something to see Karen with the baby goats, petting them, scolding one for chewing her dress, kissing them, and sweet-talking another into taking a pill. In fact, the overall feeling of the inn is crystallized when a goat walks up to you and her eyes say, Would you please scratch my head? How can you refuse?

There are other things to do at the inn besides spend time with the goats; for instance, there are two donkeys, a dock and a rowboat down on a salt marsh, and a couple of swings inside the barn with, thankfully, mosquito netting on both doors. The food is prepared by a native Maine chef who prepares a wonderfully eclectic dinner with the liberal use of herbs, fruits, and vegetables in season. The menu changes every night, and hors d'oeuvres are served at 6:30 every evening, sometimes accompanied by Bill and Karen on the player piano. A buffet breakfast is served each morning with a baked egg dish, granola, fresh fruit, juice, and yogurt. And there's a bottomless plate of chocolate chip cookies in one of the sitting rooms in the main house.

The house still contains the original wide-plank floors, beams, and fireplaces, and the inn's guest rooms—all with private bath—are furnished with period pieces. There's a serenity that emanates from the more than two-hundred-year-old walls. A line from the inn's brochure—"surround yourself with the ghosts of long contented guests"—says it all.

But still, everything comes back to the goats. "It may sound silly, but part of the reason we run the inn is to bring guests back to nature through cheese," says Bill. "Sometimes we feel like goat missionaries. After all, we have the chance to introduce three to four thousand people to goats each year."

Give it a try. It worked on me.

Karen and Bill Mitman
Squire Tarbox Inn
RR 2, Box 620
Wiscasset, ME 04578
207-882-7693
$$-$$$ bed and breakfast only, $$$ MAP
Children over 15 welcome
Open year-round

Sunset House

Sunset House also has goats, but on a much smaller scale than Squire Tarbox, and less formal as well. The late Victorian farmhouse was built in 1898 by a man with six children, so it was designed to romp around in. Attention to detail is obvious everywhere, with fresh flowers throughout including sharing space on the fireplace mantel with Hummels.

Kathy and Carl Johnson have run the Sunset House for only five years, but they say in that time they've watched the families of repeat guests grow, and they, in turn, have watched the inn change. Carl is a chef by trade, which is clearly reflected in the breakfasts at Sunset House, which range from sourdough waffles and French toast made with home-made cinnamon raisin bread, to omelets with fresh herbs from the garden. In summer, Carl makes breakfast for up to fifteen people and then goes to Bar Harbor, where he works as an executive chef. In winter, when he has four months off, he often makes dinner for guests.

Besides the food and the views—all seven rooms face the water—the animals at the small-scale farm also draw guests. Kathy raises six Alpine goats, seven ducks, and herbs and vegetables in the garden. Five of the six goats are milked, and as Kathy calls each goat's name, the animal steps up to the stanchion and starts nibbling grain. Either Kathy or her sixteen-year-old son, Mason, milks Melody, Patches, Holly, Abby, or Audrey by hand, while the sole buck—named Meat, with no pretense about his fate—stands on the sidelines.

Carl and Kathy are hospitable, and through their caring, direct manner they appear devoted to meeting every need a guest could possibly have, and even some a guest isn't aware of yet. The Johnsons are doing exactly what they want to do. As Carl put it, "B&B guests are better than having relatives visit because they're on their best behavior." Which makes meeting their needs easy.

Guests can weed the garden and even help milk the goats. Kathy says that guests first come in the barn and watch very wide-eyed and curious, then they offer to help. One family even came up during kidding season, and got everything on video while a guest caught a kid. During milking, which provides enough milk for the family and guests, the ducks come in the barn and eat up some of the grain the goats have spilled in their frenzy to get at it. The Johnson's two toy poodles, Tammy and Maggie, stand outside the barn watching passively. In short, there's a lot of activity for a small farm, but there's also a lot of nothing for guests to do as well.

Guests can use the canoe or go swimming in freshwater Jones Pond. Sunset House is on the Schoodic Peninsula, which is another quiet side of Acadia. Three of the rooms have more than one bed, and all share a bath. There's a room on the third floor of the inn where the bed faces Flander's Bay, and another where you can be the first person in the inn to see the sunrise.

The big side porch is the only side of the house that doesn't face water. But that doesn't matter; just listen to the loons call.

Kathy and Carl Johnson
Sunset House
Route 186
Gouldsboro, ME 04607
207-963-7156 or 800-233-7156
$$
Children welcome
Open year-round

Tatnic Bed & Breakfast

Don't expect a two-hundred-year-old, drafty house packed with character when you visit Tatnic Bed & Breakfast, because you won't find it. Jane and Tin Smith built their passive solar, two-thousand-square-foot house in 1980 after they attended the Shelter Institute, a house-building school up the coast in Bath, Maine. The Institute, in case you're not familiar with it, encourages people to build their dream homes themselves while incorporating into the construction environmentally sound concepts such as solar-heated water and a woodstove as the primary heat source. Tatnic stays cool in summer and warm in winter with only three and a half cords of wood.

The Shelter Institute—which I attended a number of years ago— also encourages any and every pair of hands to join in, no matter what the skill level. That served as the foundation of the B&B. "We had a dozen people sleep over every night for years when we were building the house," says Jane, "so a bed and breakfast was a natural extension of that."

The Smiths incorporated a lot of glass in the construction of their home. The better to see out from the breakfast room into the extensive flower and vegetable gardens, and watch a flock of turkeys strut around in their pen. Across the road is a small apple orchard and a buckwheat field. The Smiths board three horses—two Percheron workhorses named Ben and Jake, and their new Belgian named Krissy—at a neighbor's barn around the corner. Guests can walk up the road with Tin to feed the horses, or watch the animals at work, plowing fields or hauling a cart.

Jane says that people who are looking for something different find their way to Tatnic. A duchess visited once with her son. The woman, wearing spike heels and dripping with jewelry, walked across the footbridge that leads from the parking area over a marshy area to the house. When she opened the door to see a young-looking Tin standing there,

Percherons ready for work

she demanded in a haughty voice, "Where are your parents?" The story still makes him laugh.

"We've had a lot of people move to Maine because of us," says Jane. One of the converts was Tin's mother, Marie-Louise, who left Marblehead, Massachusetts, to live in the attached back house that Tin finished in 1988. Besides the bed and breakfast, both Jane and Tin work at home in a quilting business that includes making custom quilts for people all over the world, giving group and private lessons, selling mail-order quilting supplies, and leading an annual bus trip to Amish country, home of outstanding quilts. Jane will even give private quilting lessons to guests if they wish.

Two rooms are available for guests: one, with twin beds, is in the back of the house; the main bedroom, which looks out over the gardens, is light and airy with lots of windows. They both share a bathroom on the first floor, which has an unusual shower stall made from cement.

For breakfast, Jane serves granola, muffins, and fresh fruit. She'll give you her special granola recipe, which she layers with fresh fruit and yogurt on Sunday mornings. Everything about Tatnic is natural and inviting.

Jane and Tin Smith
Tatnic Bed & Breakfast
Box 518A
South Berwick, ME 03908
207-676-2209
$
Children welcome
Open year-round

Welchville Inn

The Welchville Inn is a good example of how farmland in New England changes, both according to the season and the fickle demands of society, while factoring in the old Yankee ethic of using what you already have. The result is a comfortable, rustic bed and breakfast with a chance for guests to witness new and old agricultural techniques that they can apply in their own gardens at home.

In summer, David and Anne Carter grow fruits and vegetables on ten acres of farmland next to the house. In winter, the Carters run a cross-country ski center over the fields and through the woods, offering miles of trails to locals and visitors who come to ski. Likewise, the enclosed farm stand that fronts onto Route 26 turns into a cross-country ski shop when the snow starts to fly.

Guests can take advantage of this dichotomy by staying in the lodge, which is an old barn that the Carters remodeled and turned into a guesthouse. The building is very rustic—yet comfortable, and the blond pine paneling is reminiscent of a Scandinavian ski lodge. On the second floor are three bedrooms with comfortable iron-frame beds. The common area near the back has a stereo and TV, and overlooks the fields. The original barn boards were used upstairs, and old beams are still visible in every room.

On the third floor is a private sleeping loft area. Remember when you were a child and you hid out in the attic, trying hard not to giggle while your mother called you to dinner? Her voice seemed to rattle the floorboards, and finally you couldn't stand it anymore and broke out with a loud laugh. That's what this huge room is like, with a separate bedroom for parents, and a couple of beds in the main area. Attic-type toys are up here, too, such as a small pool table and a few old board games.

The Carters' three daughters—Jessica, Sarah, and Emily—help out in the garden and in the house, but they don't like to do it all the time, and many times guests are happy to oblige.

Anne tells of one couple who came to stay at the inn for a few days. "They wanted to pick corn in the worst way, since they had never done it before," she says. "So they rode with David on the truck during the harvest, and when they left we gave them a whole bushel of corn to take back with them. That's the kind of thing they remember year after year. Another time there was a boy from New York who came to visit, and at first, he wanted to help, but then after a while, he didn't want to do it anymore."

Anne serves a full country breakfast in the main house, where the family lives. In summer she specializes in making elaborate omelets using just-picked vegetables from the garden. After breakfast, and at night, guests tend to congregate in the common areas in the lodge, not the house.

"With children," says Anne, "there's too much going on, and we can keep a separate B&B area cleaner and less cluttered. Our place isn't as fancy as other places, but some people like it more because they feel they can relax.

"A lot of families who have been guests at Welchville invite us to their homes. In fact, last summer a couple from New York came with their child, who got attached to my youngest daughter. The mother sent books to our children, and we wrote back and forth. They invited us to come stay with them, and last year, we went to their house in Manhattan for spring vacation."

Anne and David Carter
Welchville Inn
RR 1, Box 710
Oxford, ME 04270
207-539-4848
$$
Children welcome
Open year-round

MASSACHUSETTS

Canterbury Farm
Becket

Cumworth Farm
Cummington

Penfrydd Farm Bed & Breakfast
Colrain

Steep Acres Farm
Williamstown

Canterbury Farm

Canterbury Farm, a short drive from Tanglewood, Jacob's Pillow Dance Festival, and a number of other Berkshire attractions, was Linda Bacon's summer house as a child. She's still as excited about it today as she was when she and her husband, David, first started the bed and breakfast in 1985. A little enthusiasm goes a long way in this business.

Linda's parents bought the farm in 1940, and decided to sell it in the early eighties. At that time, Linda had been footloose, traveling all over the country, and was ready to come back to the Berkshires and live year-round in the house. Once she returned, she read her parents' accounts of the time they spent at the farm, and discovered that they used to fix up one room in the 210-year-old house each year. Today, Linda and David are doing the same thing.

Like many modern farmers, the Bacons do a little bit of everything. Canterbury is a two-hundred-acre tree farm, and since David works as a landscaper, he grows many different kinds of trees for his customers on the land. The farm has been carefully managed under a forest conservation plan since the 1930s, and offers a series of hiking trails in summer that turn into an extensive cross-country ski system in winter. The elevation at the farm is seventeen hundred feet, so when roads in the valley have sparse snowfall, it's usually abundant at the farm.

Dave also plays in a band, and squeezed into the room off the breakfast room is a baby grand piano, a set of drums, and a flute. The braided rug on the floor was made by Linda's mother, along with all the other rugs in the house. She's seventy-nine and still visits the farm and makes rugs for it. Linda pointed out the remnants of a wool plaid jacket in the living room rug that she'd worn as a child in the sixties.

Linda has two small boys who look wide-eyed at every new guest who arrives at the farm, and she also teaches elementary school. She says that having guests at the farm can sometimes be like having small children, what with all the questions they ask. While she's making breakfast, sit down at the small bar in the breakfast room and have your first cup of coffee while she chats with you. Blueberry pancakes, omelets, or Linda's special egg and bacon bake are favorites.

There are four guest rooms at Canterbury; the most popular is on the first floor with a private bath and a fireplace. Three rooms upstairs share a large, carpeted bath. All of the rooms have comfortable beds, antique furniture, decorative oil lamps, and, of course, braided rugs. It's quiet at the farm—after all, trees don't make much noise—and after breakfast, even though I had slept soundly, I felt as though I had to take a nap. And so it was, out to the hammock in the garden.

Besides walking through the perennial gardens or lingering by the small pond, guests have access to a public beach at Center Pond nearby. In summer, Linda takes her children almost every day.

Linda and David Bacon
Canterbury Farm
Fred Snow Road
Becket, MA 01223
413-623-8765
$$
Children welcome
Open year-round

Cumworth Farm

Cumworth Farm is a mirror of its owners in its diversity: there's a little bit of everything here.

Ed and Mary McColgan started working their twenty-five-acre farm in 1979 in between Ed's position as a history professor, serving three terms in the state legislature, running the Massachusetts bicentennial commission, and, finally, working with various state public health departments.

Today, Cumworth has two calves, six sheep, two Scottish Highland cattle, a beefalo, and a steer. Barn cats, as usual, wander around the farm. Nell, the farm's pedigree border collie, loves to play with any children in the vicinity. There's a pick-your-own raspberry and blueberry farm, and the McColgans operate an extensive maple sugaring business, producing five hundred gallons of syrup each season. They also grow all their own vegetables.

"If guests want to help out, we'll find something for them to do," says Ed. He adds, however, that many people with the best of intentions never get past the outdoor hot tub, which he built a couple of years ago. Children who visit like to help feed the animals, but sometimes their parents have different ideas of what to do on a farm. Ed tells about one man who had slept out in the hay as a child. When he visited Cumworth with his own children, he insisted that they all sleep out in the barn in the hay. The next morning, the children felt itchy. The father looked as though he'd had a better time than his children.

The McColgans just finished their twelfth season of running the bed and breakfast. They've received guests who spent days at farm chores and others who were musicians at nearby Tanglewood and who practiced on the farm's spinet in the living room.

The history of the farm is equally diverse. The part of the house that accommodates the kitchen and TV room was built in 1780; the rest of the house was built in 1804. The barn board in the kitchen came from a dismantled barn that was formerly on the land. The family that built the house then began a dairy farm and continued farming until the Depression, when they lost the farm. The next owner started an apple orchard in the 1940s, but the land was rarely farmed until the McColgans took it over. In a nod to modern times, they put in a solar hot-water system.

The barn—where the man and his children slept—is a fine example of pre-Civil War construction, and it's still in good shape. Built in the 1840s, it is fastened with only pegs and no nails in the post-and-beam construction. The flagstone foundation doesn't have a drop of cement; it's held together by gravity and judicious placement. The barn was once used for apple storage; today Ed uses it as a sheep pen. On the second floor, there are trapdoors all over the floor to throw hay down to the animals below. As farming in New England has changed, so have the barns.

In the main house there are six bedrooms for guests, with ceiling fans and well-stocked bookcases in every room. For breakfast, Mary makes pancakes served with the farm's own maple syrup. Try to have breakfast in the kitchen in summer to watch the hummingbirds and house finches that congregate outside.

Mary and Ed McColgan
Cumworth Farm
472 W. Cummington Road
Cummington, MA 01026
413-634-5529
$$
Children welcome
Open year-round

Penfrydd Farm Bed & Breakfast

Penfrydd is simply magical. It's not easy to find—it's way out in the country—but it's worth it to meet Thom and Ceacy Griffin and their menagerie of eccentric animals.

Penfrydd is primarily a llama farm, with twenty to twenty-five of the camelids wandering around at any one time. Ceacy's been raising llamas for ten years for their fleece, and today she still sells fleece, but also hand-dyed yarn, and animals for pets and breeding services.

"People come here for the llamas," she says, though once they arrive, they discover that the farm's five ducks, five dogs, two cats, twelve sheep, one goat, two Jersey calves, ten Norwegian Fjord horses, and a miniature donkey provide enough entertainment so that there's no need to weave their way back to civilization. The Griffins also plan to get some chickens.

The Griffins spend a lot of time with guests on their 160-acre farm. "We spend lots of time answering questions and helping people interact with the animals," says Ceacy. "People don't want to just look at the animals over a fence. Llamas are so unusual that people wait patiently for me to come over and introduce them to the animals, one by one."

Thom grew up on a farm, and Ceacy raised sheep when she was a teenager. All along, she knew she wanted to have her own farm, and became interested in llamas because of their wool. She also had horses years ago, and only recently renewed her interest, to take a breather from the farm. Norwegian Fjords are beautiful tan horses with an unusual mane that stands straight up like a Mohawk and is white with a thin black stripe running down the middle. "You can't go very far on a farm," Ceacy says, so she goes out riding in the woods for a few hours a day. She frequently takes guests out on cart rides with the horses or llama treks for a tour of the farm.

Guests who want to help out with farm chores can brush and feed the horses and other animals, and clean out the stalls. Thom jokes that

Fjords bring in the wood

they give special discounts for weight lifters. Much of farm work is physically tough, though, and guests can just follow along if they'd like.

Penfrydd is named after a Welsh manor where Thom's ancestors lived before they came to America. The Griffins have lived in the 160-year-old house for eight years; they started the bed and breakfast in 1992 when a man from the local land trust suggested it. The house is a curious combination of old and new: Thom and Ceacy totally renovated the house with new sheetrock and windows, but kept the old post and beams. They also added a new deck that looks out onto the llama pasture. If llamas are new to you, all conversation will probably cease when you catch one of the animals casually walking by. They're beautiful, self-assured creatures that are fascinating to watch.

The three guest rooms are upstairs; the room with a private bath has a Jacuzzi, a skylight above the bed, and lots of angles that point out the original construction of the house. It's a huge room with a bay window where you can sit and survey the calf pen.

Ceacy offers guests a breakfast buffet or full breakfast by request. Full breakfast includes fresh fruit and yogurt, scrambled eggs with herbs, pancakes, bacon, and freshly baked bread.

A small shop is attached to the house where Ceacy's hand-dyed yarns are sold, as well as handmade sweaters. And there's a flower garden outside the back door. The Griffins do their own haying, which makes me think, how do they do it all and still be so pleasant to their guests?

"We see the B&B as an opportunity to educate people about farming, the good and the bad," she says.

Ceacy and Thom Griffin
Penfrydd Farm Bed & Breakfast
RR 1, Box 100A
Colrain, MA 01340
413-624-5516
$$
Children welcome
Open year-round

Steep Acres Farm

Steep Acres lives up to its name. After you pass through the center of Williamstown and drive through a suburban setting, it's straight up the driveway to the fifty-acre farm. Since you're at the top of the mountain, you can't hear the sound of the traffic from town and Route 7 just a mile away.

Steep Acres boasts the only diving board in Williamstown on the farm's large man-made pond down a knoll from the main house. You could spend all day down here, with a small beach, picnic tables and chairs, a canoe and kayak, and a floating lounge chair for the ultimate in relaxation. There's also a tetherball, a volleyball net, and even a couple of trampolines. There are bird feeders all over the place, and a couple of duck houses that float on the pond and are home to a few mallards.

Back at the house, a bevy of dogs—from five to seven Labs at any one time—greet you and serve as your escorts as you walk around the farm. Across the dirt road is a barn that houses a sole pig and a few chickens. Hosts Mary and Marvin Gangemi also keep a few bees for honey.

They've been farming Steep Acres for more than a decade, and started taking in guests when their six children began to leave home. One son, however, just moved across the street; he works as a landscaper and designed and maintains the extensive gardens that surround the house.

The house has four guest rooms that share two baths: a room with a twin bed, another with two twins, and two doubles. There are fresh flowers and a dish of candy in every room, and antique trunks at the foot of the double beds. You'll see cute miniature door knockers on the way into each room. If you can, try to reserve the double with the half-bath. The room has a magnificent queen-sized bed with a towering hand-carved headboard and an ornate marble-topped cottage pine dresser that matches the bed's headboard. Lace throw pillows cover the bed, and the bath has lights over the vanity.

But what's outside the window is the room's best feature, with views that look onto the orchard and far pasture, and west to the Adirondacks. Sharing the view is a screened porch, furnished with white wicker chairs and sofas, plenty of books, and two hanging cages with canaries.

Mary serves a full breakfast and never the same thing twice—unless you ask for it. In summer, guests eat breakfast outside at tables on the grassy terrace.

The living room and dining room each have their own fireplace, with plenty of chairs gathered around for winter in this brown-shingled, weathered house that is just two miles from Williams College.

Mary and Marvin Gangemi
Steep Acres Farm
520 White Oaks Road
Williamstown, MA 01267
413-458-3774
$-$$
Children welcome
Open year-round

A friendly farm dog at Steep Acres

NEW HAMPSHIRE

Darby Brook Farm
Alstead

Ellis River House
Jackson

Honey Lane Farm
Dublin

The Inn at East Hill Farm
Troy

Nestlenook Farm
Jackson Village

Peep Willow Farm
Marlborough

Rockhouse Mountain Farm
Eaton Center

Wild Goose Farm
Northwood

Windyledge Bed & Breakfast
Hopkinton

Darby Brook Farm

Some have said that walking into the ten-room, two-hundred-year-old farmhouse at Darby Brook Farm is like walking into a museum. I'll take it one step further: it's like stepping into the nineteenth century with the convenience of twentieth-century plumbing and electricity.

If you're used to antique-filled inns with plush carpeting and polished woodwork, Darby Brook Farm is a hefty dose of how it really was for most families back in the early days of this country's history. Owner Howard Weeks—who spent his summers in this family home—has furnished the farmhouse with local period furniture. Original stenciling borders the plaster walls, and old prints—some framed, others tacked directly to the walls—are found throughout the house. The wide-board floors are painted. A stuffed owl stands on the sideboard to greet you when you first walk in. Bird prints, old clocks, decoys, and family paintings and photographs adorn the walls. There's even a map of the American Republic from 1844, when Iowa was as far west as it went.

There are three bed-and-breakfast rooms that share a large bath with a clawfoot tub, and two of the guest rooms have their own fireplaces. The doors to the bathroom have old-fashioned latches on them that serve as locks. Just remember to flip them back when you leave.

Weeks has been farming a two-acre plot on his twenty-three acres for the eleven years that he's been living here year-round. He started the bed and breakfast—open May through October—at about the same time. He cultivates vegetables such as broccoli, cabbage, and eggplant, which he sells from a cart in front of the house, as well as at a farmers' market down in Keene. He also provides pick-your-own strawberry and raspberry patches and maintains a ten-acre hayfield. Weeks plants and harvests his crops in much the same way as the people who lived in the house one and two centuries ago—by hand.

The vegetable fields are at the foot of a slightly rolling meadow behind the house; a small apple orchard stands at the top of the hill, guarded by a solar electric fence to keep the deer from nibbling the fruit. Mowed walking trails line the perimeter of the fields, and lead to more trails farther up in the woods. Weeks keeps some chickens, sheep, and turkeys near the garden. Queenie the dog and Barney the cat round out the animal life.

Weeks closes the bed and breakfast in winter because it's not insulated, and moves into a heated studio apartment above the garage. His father bought the farm in 1929, and Howard inherited it in 1981. Since this area of the state is not heavily touristed, most of the guests who stay at the farm have a local connection: either they're visiting relatives in the area or they've lived here in the past. The lack of traffic and tourists doesn't bother Howard. If you want a glimpse into how a small farm was run a century ago, and an authentic-looking house, Darby Brook is the place.

Howard Weeks
Darby Brook Farm
Hill Road
Alstead, NH 03602
603-835-6624
$$
Children welcome
Open May through October

Ellis River House

As you push your way north on Route 16 through North Conway, the outlet capital of New Hampshire, you might look at the cars from every state but the Granite State and despair of ever seeing a farm within a fifty-mile radius of the town.

Be patient and continue on to Jackson, one town north of the sprawl. The Ellis River House, a large bed-and-breakfast inn with a small farm, seems miles away from Outlet Center USA. Owners Barbara and Barry Lubao have just put the finishing touches on a fourteen-room addition to the inn's original seven guest rooms, and such amenities as working fireplaces and two-person Jacuzzi bathroom spas combine nicely with the pony, ducks, chicken, geese, and a pig named Stimpy out in the barn.

The main Colonial farmhouse was built in 1893; the Lubaos have been running the inn for eight years, which is a couple of years past the average commitment for an innkeeping couple. Running Ellis River House must still seem like somewhat of a vacation to Barry, since he spent a number of years as chief engineer at a Sheraton hotel. While he worked for someone else, he'd always dreamed of owning his own hotel, and judging by the recent expansion to the inn, he's hit on a formula that works.

The guest rooms are decorated with antique furnishings and country fabrics. A soft terrycloth robe hangs in the closet of each room. The bedrooms at the back of the house overlook the Ellis River, and if you sleep with the windows open, you'll doze off to the sound of gurgling water that rushes fast and furious in spring and slows to a bare trickle in late summer. A second-story deck overlooks the river. The north side of the house offers a good view of Mount Washington.

The inn's Jacuzzi is in a large, bright, wood-paneled room filled with windows and plants. You might have the spa to yourself in summer, but be prepared to wait in winter, because skiers who stay at the inn spend their apres-ski time in the tub as they wait for Barry to ring the dinner bell. Dinner—available for a fee—is served by candlelight and is open to guests by reservation. The menu includes an appetizer, homemade soup or a salad, an entree, home-baked breads, and dessert. Entrees might include glazed duck for two, lobster, or baked stuffed haddock. The next morning, Barry cooks breakfast to order: eggs any style—which guests can collect for themselves that morning in the henhouse—and pancakes are standard offerings, along with a thick slice of homemade cinnamon bread.

Dinner and breakfast are served in the dining room in the main house; wing chairs, a woodstove, old clocks, and a baby grand piano adorn the room. You'll find knickknacks, both old and new, all through the inn. From an old William Tell bank to vintage tobacco cans and family pictures, every square inch of space is spoken for, without seeming cluttered.

In addition to the twenty-one inn rooms, there's a small two-room cottage next to the barn that formerly served as an icehouse. Downstairs there's a small sitting room with a dining table, microwave oven, and TV. The spiral staircase leads up to the bedroom, where a curved window over the bed looks out to the river. Many honeymooners and couples away for a romantic weekend have booked the icehouse.

I visited Ellis River House in summer, but it is even more enticing in winter, to spend bright, cold days skiing or shopping, and then come back to this cocoon and hibernate for the rest of the evening, in front of your own private fireplace in your room, or beside one of several other hearths throughout the common area in the inn.

Barbara and Barry Lubao
Ellis River House
Box 656
Jackson, NH 03846
603-383-9339 or 800-233-8309
$$-$$$, dinner optional
Children welcome
Open year-round

Honey Lane Farm

Honey Lane Farm is first and foremost a horse farm, but "nonriders," as horse people call them, always with a bit of amazement, are also welcome here.

Al and Aline Coutu run a variety of programs for riders of all abilities at the farm. Summertime is devoted to horsemanship camp for children. The Coutus take boys age seven through twelve and girls seven through sixteen years of age. Beginning through advanced riders spend one, two, or four weeks at the camp learning the basic skills and everything from show jumping to dressage, with special visits from a veterinarian and a blacksmith. Some campers even bring their own horses.

The country's two largest equestrian tour agencies, Equitour and Fits Equestrian, regularly run week-long tours through the Mount Monadnock region, with Honey Lane Farm as the base. All levels of riders learn proper horse grooming and riding techniques, and how to tack a horse. The features of the week are the trail rides in the area that take riders on logging roads, through dense forest, and into abandoned towns that are accessible only by foot or—better—by horse. Three meals a day are included, with lunch on the trail and breakfast and dinner back at the lodge.

Al is the chef at Honey Lane, before which he spent twenty-five years in the restaurant business. Aline says that preparing a lunch buffet in the woods and providing cheese and crackers for riders at the end of the day have been one long vacation for him.

The flexible programs at Honey Lane include a number of weekends in spring and fall, in which guests spend Friday through Sunday on two trail rides—after an evaluation and proper match with a horse—and tennis, fishing, swimming, hiking, golfing, or just relaxing the rest of the time. Full-week programs at Honey Lane follow the same concept, except that they run Saturday through Saturday during selected weeks in spring and fall.

Honey Lane's stationary program is ideal for people who are novices who want to learn the basics and for more advanced riders who want to brush up on their skills. Frequently, experienced riders use the stationary program to get into shape for a future trek or to prepare for showing. This is total immersion in the equestrian life: participants get a horse for the duration of their stay that they are responsible for grooming, tacking, and feeding, along with a daily lesson and trail ride. Participating in the care and feeding of the horse is a required part of the program. Everyone does it gladly.

Everything at Honey Lane is geared toward equestrians, from the swimming pool that's open in summer, to a year-round outdoor Jacuzzi on the deck of the main lodge, to the services of an on-call massage therapist. In winter, the horses at Honey Lane still keep busy, because Girl Scout troops from all over New England spend a weekend at the farm to earn their horse lover's badge; some come back every year, even though they've earned several badges already.

Mrs. Aline Coutu
Honey Lane Farm
Box 353
Dublin, NH 03444
603-563-8078
$$$ AP
Children welcome
Open year-round

The Inn at East Hill Farm

The brochure for the Inn at East Hill Farm reads "Where Kids Are Kings." Fortunately for families, they really mean it.

In summer, hosts Dave and Sally Adams say that a family could spend a week at the farm and easily never leave the premises, with the meals, activities, and company that are provided. It's a combination of a day camp for children and a relaxing vacation for their parents. There's nothing fancy about the 150-acre farm, but the Adamses make no pretense about it. The accommodations range from private two-bedroom cabins with private bath and sitting area, to single guest rooms in the main house, to motel-like rooms in a newer building called Trailsend.

Collecting the eggs

Wander through the various outbuildings and barns and you'll see all the traditional farm animals, close enough for children to step up and get a good look and even pet. Pigs, horses, sheep, cows, goats, chickens, and even grouse and pheasant share space. Children can collect hens' eggs and bring them to the cook for their breakfast.

One price includes a room and three meals a day, making it easy for families to stay, since even the meals are geared toward families and children with fussy appetites. The food is plentiful and delicious: at every meal there's something unusual, such as potato pancakes at breakfast served alongside eggs, regular pancakes, and cereal. Blueberry fritters with real maple syrup is one of the appetizers at dinner. We were told that an outdoor lunch would consist of hot dogs and hamburgers, but it turned out to be much more than that, with soup, salad, fruit, beef burgundy, macaroni and cheese, chicken stir-fry, and then, finally, the grill with the burgers and dogs. By then, there was no more room on the plate.

The farm is sprawling, yet self-contained. An outdoor pool sits near the main farmhouse, with a sandbox, swings, volleyball net, and plenty of lawn chairs set up to face massive Mount Monadnock in the background. The mountain doesn't seem real; rather, it looks as though someone painted a mural and slapped it up in the sky. In the marsh area, where paddleboats and rowboats are available for guests to use, the mountain seems even more surreal.

Shuffleboard courts, tennis courts, pony rides, hay rides, horseback riding, walking trails, and nearby golf courses and bowling alleys add to the diversity of activities. A few miles away, at the farm's cottage on Silver Lake, guests can go swimming, fishing, and water-skiing. On rainy days, like any good summer camp, there are plenty of indoor activities. There's a lounge in the basement of the main house with a Ping-Pong table, a pinball machine, video machines, a pool table, and an indoor pool. Capacity at the height of summer can reach 120 guests, with half of them children, so people who prefer solitude might want to choose winter to stay at the farm.

Cross-country ski trails ring the land, and an enclosed skating rink is on the premises. Sleigh rides are also available, and the staff provides the evening's entertainment most nights. In spring and fall, Dave and Sally host many square-dance weekends. The farm is open year-round, with two special fall weekends that are especially popular: a foliage weekend in late September, and Family Weekend on Columbus Day weekend.

Sally and Dave Adams
The Inn at East Hill Farm
Troy, NH 03465
603-242-6495 or 800-242-6495
$ AP
Children welcome
Open year-round

Nestlenook Farm

Spending the night at Nestlenook Farm is like stepping into a Currier and Ives painting. Originally built as a robber baron's gentleman's farm back in 1890, this exquisitely decorated two-hundred-year-old inn on sixty-five acres is a complete throwback to Victorian days.

Nestlenook is the oldest house in Jackson. Appropriately, you reach the farm by driving through a historic red covered bridge. The inn has seven luxuriously decorated rooms, all named after notable artists who worked in the Mount Washington Valley, where Nestlenook is located; a painting by each hangs in the room named for them. Some of the guest rooms are furnished with hand-carved canopy beds and nineteenth-century cast-iron parlor stoves. One room has a fireplace with a mantle made of cherry and a balcony where you can walk out and survey the land. In one of the rooms, there's an antique chiming mantle clock. Each room has a private bath with a two-person Jacuzzi tub.

Downstairs, the parlor room contains an antique black wrought-iron bird cage complete with six chirping finches that serenade guests each morning. The adjacent breakfast room features a tin ceiling that's original to the house, as well as an authentic reproduction of the famous Count Rumford fireplace.

Owners Robert and Nancy Cyr bought Nestlenook in 1989 and proceeded to spend a year and a half renovating it. Their aim throughout the arduous process was to provide the ultimate in romantic getaways for their guests. They've succeeded, inside and out.

Admittedly, Nestlenook is not what you think of when you use the word *farm*, but there are enough animals here to keep farm-minded guests happy. Jet and Lacey are miniature Nordic horses, and Nestle and Nook are the inn's resident Clydesdales. Prancer and Donner—reindeer, of course—are kept in a penned-in area on the far edge of the main grounds. In winter, when families from the area come to the inn for a sleigh ride, children can get out when they reach the reindeer pen and feed the animals handfuls of grain through the fence. Two other horses—Justin, who's thirty, and Thunder, a mere five years old—graze nearby, and three sheep—Baba, Daisy, and Sheba—have free rein of the property. There are also a couple of rabbits in the horse stables, and rainbow trout in the stocked pond.

The grounds at Nestlenook contain immaculately tended flower gardens, an outdoor swimming pool, an elegant fountain, a formal courtyard, and the pond, where you can ice skate under the gently curving pedestrian bridge. Cross-country skiers who use the trails that weave through the woods can spend time in a warming hut in the form of a gazebo.

Other special amenities at Nestlenook include a kitchen especially for guests, where teas, cocoa, coffee, and popcorn are always available. The kitchen's highlight is an original Belanger reconditioned stove from before the turn of the century; it still has its original tiles intact.

In the TV room in the basement is a fifty-inch television with surround sound and a laser disc machine with more than sixty new and recent movies to choose from. There's also a pool table, dart board, and woodstove.

Lionel is the innkeeper at Nestlenook: he checks you in, shows you to your room, and makes breakfast—pancakes, waffles, and omelets—prepared with little fat. On summer afternoons, he serves wine and cheese on the screened patio just off the breakfast room, which has a resident chipmunk, another one of Nestlenook's animals. In winter, Lionel will toss out a scoop of granola to feed Chippy; in summer, he'll throw out four scoops, to keep the chipmunk off the tables.

Nancy and Robert Cyr
Nestlenook Farm
Dinsmore Road
Jackson Village, NH 03846
603-383-9443
$$$
Children over 12 welcome
Open year-round

Peep Willow Farm

"There's always something to do at a farm," says Noel Aderer of Peep Willow Farm, who half-jokes, "There is no extra charge for helping with the farm chores."

Peep Willow Farm was named after two of Noel's thoroughbred horses. Guests who want to keep busy can brush and feed the horses, help during haying season, and lead a horse to pasture. All of the horses at the farm have been raised by children, with Noel's help, so the animals are all very people oriented. Noel regularly invites guests down to the barn to pet the horses and talk to them.

However, her horses are not the common equestrian variety; rather, Noel refers to them as the Ferraris of the horse world. All of them are thoroughbreds, either in training or active competition, and they're very large: some are more than sixteen hands high. In addition to guests, Noel also accepts apprentices who stay at the farm and receive a lesson every day in exchange for a fee and taking care of the horses. Noel will also board other people's horses, but the focus is on her Ferraris, named Mikey, Peeper, and Froggy, the last so named because of her big hind legs.

In spring, there are always at least a couple of foals at the farm, and guests like to sit in the living room with the big picture window that over-looks the pasture and just watch the antics.

Noel has been living on the seventeen-acre farm, just down the road from Mount Monadnock, since 1980, and opened the bed and breakfast a year later. She says that all types of people stay at the farm, from those who are completely indifferent toward animals, to equestrians who bring their own horses and ride the surrounding trails for a week. Unlike many farms, she lets guests bring their well-behaved dogs, though they have to stay on a leash until they prove themselves. "I travel with dogs," she says, "and on occasion I've had to sneak them in where I was staying, so I let them come to the farm." One time, she says, someone even brought a cat.

On summer weekends, Noel is away from the farm competing,

You can help during haying

serving as a competition official, or running her own competition at a farm down the road, so breakfast for guests on those mornings tends to be the self-help variety: she leaves fruit, cereal, coffee, eggs, and other provisions for guests to prepare themselves. She's usually around in summer during the week. If guests have no plans for dinner, she will invite them for a cookout. Noel is around more in winter. "I'll sit down all morning and talk with guests," she says, undoubtedly over French toast made from her homemade bread with maple syrup from the sugarbush on the farm.

Meals are served at a long picnic table in the kitchen. Downstairs, there's a sitting room with a woodstove, and around the corner is a fireplace in the room with the large picture window. There are three guest rooms at Peep Willow. The downstairs bedroom, at the corner of the house, has two twin beds. Windows on each wall provide a view of the pasture and the woods. Upstairs are two more guest rooms, one with a king-sized bed, another with a double. Wide-plank floors are all through the house with worn-away patches in areas of heavy traffic.

Guests come back again and again, and staple their business cards in Noel's guest book. A black German shepherd named Splash wanders around the grounds. Barnum, a Morris clone, has the official title of Farm Manager. "Nothing gets past him," she says of the cat. "When new guests come up the driveway, he seems to ask, Are these electric blanket guests, or do they prefer a cat? And he always pegs them just right.

"We do what we can when we can," she says. "In my whole life, I never dreamed of having a place like this. I'm lucky and I love to share it. And if I was wealthy, I wouldn't charge a thing."

Noel Aderer
Peep Willow Farm
Marlborough, NH 03455
603-876-3807
$
Children welcome
Open year-round

Rockhouse Mountain Farm

Whenever a guest leaves Rockhouse Mountain Farm at the end of a vacation, whether it's one night or one week, the entire staff comes out to the front door and rings a variety of handbells as a send-off. It's a touching gesture, even after a brief stay.

But I'm getting ahead of myself. Rockhouse Mountain Farm is like summer camp for the whole family, with activities that include hikes to the Indian caves on the farm's 450 acres to a weekly cookout at the Swift River on Tuesdays complete with grilled hamburgers and, later, a swim at the waterfall.

Rockhouse has been run by the same family for forty-seven years. Libby Edge, age seventy-nine, who started the resort with her late husband, John, now runs the farm with her son Johnny. She says that some of the guests at Rockhouse have been coming for almost as long as the resort has existed.

In fact, longevity is the rule at the farm, not the exception. Children from different families hook up over one weekend, and become pen pals. They then easily convince both sets of parents to come back to Rockhouse the same week the next year. Employees come back, too. Libby tells of one employee whose grandparents started coming to the farm in the fifties. The granddaughter came to Rockhouse for the first time in 1978 when she was five years old, and she hasn't missed a summer since. She just completed her third summer as an employee.

The farm is open from mid-June through the beginning of November. It can accommodate up to fifty guests at a time in the main farmhouse, which dates from the turn of the century, or the 20 House, which the Edges built in their twentieth season on the farm. There are also a couple of cabins available for families, who provide the bulk of the guests at Rockhouse.

It's no surprise. There's a two-hundred-year-old barn that shelters a hodgepodge of animals—pigs, horses, and cows; there's a field for llamas across the road, and there are lots of kittens and dogs. Libby tells the story about a little girl who overheard Johnny and Libby talking about getting the cows bred. "Well, she scooted out of here and went to her mother and told her, all excited, that we were feeding the cows bread."

Perhaps the most unusual animals at Rockhouse are the peacocks. They wander around and call to each other frequently during the day. At first, I thought it was a cat with unusually large vocal cords—until I looked out the window and saw a luminous peacock with his feathers fully spread and strutting his stuff. Another called back from the other side of the farmyard. One sounded as though he was saying, Come on, come on, while the other sounded as though he was meowing. This goes on all day.

Guests like to help out with cutting and pitching the hay, and the children like to collect eggs. The farm is not far from the hundreds of outlet stores in North Conway, though Johnny says, "We get mad when people come here to go outlet shopping because there's so much to do here."

Eating is one of those things. Besides the Tuesday cookout, there's

A charming pile of pink piglets

74

a Saturday night steak roast and a chicken barbecue on Wednesdays at the sugarhouse, and all of them have lots of food. Corn pudding, breads, salads, vegetables, and more accompany the main meals, served every night, all of them made with Libby's recipes.

The dynamics at Rockhouse are such that everyone becomes friendly with everyone else right away. There's no check-in or check-out time; people come here because they want to be here, and it's the same for the people who work here.

So try not to think it's corny when they ring the bells for you.

Libby and Johnny Edge
Rockhouse Mountain Farm
Eaton Center, NH 03832
603-447-2880
$$ MAP
Children welcome
Open mid-June through early November

Wild Goose Farm

Wild Goose Farm is the only farm in this book that has a phone in the bathroom. But don't worry, it's not *that* kind of place. Owner David Cody couldn't live without a phone in the bathroom, so when he first remodeled the house, that was one of his top priorities, besides having an indoor bathroom at all, along with central heating, both of which the house lacked.

The farm is a few miles from busy Route 4, which serves as a kind of antique alley in the town of Northwood. Once you get to the farm, however, it's easy to hide out from the world. In fact, a few have. One man came for a month to work on his doctorate, bringing several computers and suitcases full of papers. "He never went out," says David, which, given the layout of the house, is easy to do.

In the guest room that has a fireplace there's an antique canopy bed with fabric draped around each corner and again across the top. It was one of the most comfortable beds I ever slept in, and it was with great reluctance that I finally dragged myself out. In fact, David says that people frequently linger in the house for the whole day. They eat breakfast— David serves fresh fruit in a goblet, cream and sugar in an antique silver set, homemade breads with jams and jellies he's made himself, and eggs from the farm's two chickens—and then light a fire in the fireplace, and go back to bed and spend the day dozing and reading.

It's easy to see why: the dozen geese out in the pen are silent until a stranger—you—nears the pen. Immediately, a cacophony of honking starts. They lower their necks close to the ground and start banging their beaks against the fence, hoping to get near you. If you try to soothe them, it makes it worse. Only when David says, "Okay, guys," and you walk away does the noise cease.

Besides running the farm and B&B, David is also an antique dealer, and has furnished the house with old furniture and knickknacks that look so unusual that you just have to ask what that thing leaning up against the fireplace was supposed to do. That, he'll say, is a bean flailer, and then proceed to demonstrate how it works. The swiveling drying rack on either side of the fireplace was draped with cloth and was used to shelter the fire from drafts. And the wooden pegs that jut out of the original beams were used to hang up everything from food to candles, in order to protect them from the rodents.

Chinese vases, pewter pots, baskets, mugs, and an old bellows all perch on shelves in the living room above the fireplace and in the kitchen. Sometimes, a guest will admire a pair of candlesticks and end up buying them.

David is a tenth-generation American; his ancestors came over from Wales in 1698. The dark portraits in the corner are of his great-grand-fathers, who were both in the shipping business. Their eyes seem to follow you around the room.

The house itself, along with its contents, has a rich history. It was built in 1767 by Caleb Clough, a soldier in the revolutionary war, whose grave is across the street in a small cemetery that David maintains. During the Civil War, a couple of sisters whose husbands went off to fight lived in the house. It's rumored they got bored and started to entertain various men who passed by. One day, a tin salesman went up to the house and was never heard from again. Many years later, his gear was dug up in the yard. Even today, locals say that on cold winter nights you can hear the rattle of tin as the wind blows through the trees.

David Cody
Wild Goose Farm
RFD 1, Box 3205
Northwood, NH 03261
603-942-5593
$$
Children welcome
Open year-round

Windyledge Bed & Breakfast

Windyledge has twelve chickens, two barn cats, one old horse, and three guest rooms that Dick and Susan Vogt opened to the public three years ago when their last daughter went off to college. As such, it has the feel of a house that is fully used by a family; for example, there's a heated outdoor swimming pool. But it has the kinds of touches that come only from years of raising children by parents who, through trial and error, have learned to anticipate their children's every need. For instance, if each child wants a different kind of soap, a wide assortment is provided, as well as a cabinet full of toiletries for you to use if you left anything at home. Windyledge succeeds nicely on this account, along with the TV and VCR downstairs with 130 movies to choose from; everyone can find at least one to agree on.

Windyledge is only fifteen minutes from Concord, sharing a quiet road with a couple of large farms. It's not considered a tourist area; many guests come to the state capital on business or have children who are students at New England College in Henniker, the next town. The New Hampshire International Speedway in nearby Loudon fills every room in the vicinity of twenty miles on busy race weekends.

"I make no excuse about the cholesterol and calories at breakfast," says Dick, and the meal lives up to his word, starting with fruit in season with heavy cream, and perhaps a sour cream souffle with raspberry sauce or a German apple pancake served with sausage on the side. When the Vogts decided to open the bed and breakfast, Dick spent several months developing a variety of breakfast menus, and then regularly invited friends and family to try out the recipes. Eventually he built up a repertoire of gourmet dishes, and his vegetable frittatas and apricot-glazed French toast regularly get oohs and aahs from guests around the breakfast table.

The food helps break the ice among couples staying at the inn to whom the B&B experience is new; Dick says that two couples who met at breakfast one morning at Windyledge went on a bicycle trip to Paris later that year.

The living room has a piano with photos of all the Vogts' children on top, along with the exchange students who spent a year living in the house. "We've always had extra people living here," says Dick, which led to their decision to open the house to guests. There are plenty of books along with Dick's collection of old wood and brass hand tools.

The three guest rooms at Windyledge are each named for a different distinguishing feature of the room. The Pine Room, with a private bath, is named after its queen-sized pine pencil-post bed. The Country Room is decorated in the rural style and shares a bath with the International Room across the hall, which housed the international exchange students who regularly passed through the Vogts' door. The International Room features an antique Victorian double bed with a massive handmade headboard and an Oriental rug.

Dick and Susan enjoy running the bed and breakfast, and they say they're going to run it for a few more years before they take off for a while and travel.

Susan and Dick Vogt
Windyledge Bed & Breakfast
Hatfield Road, RFD #3
Hopkinton, NH 03229
603-746-4054
$$
Children welcome
Open year-round

VERMONT

Broadview Farm Bed & Breakfast
St. Johnsbury

Harvey's Mountain View Inn & Farm
Rochester

Hill Farm Inn
Arlington

Hivue Bed & Breakfast
Brandon

Homeplace
Jericho

Hound's Folly
Mount Holly

Knoll Farm Country Inn
Waitsfield

Lake Ledge Farm
Orwell

Lareau Farm Country Inn
Waitsfield

Liberty Hill Farm
Rochester

Maple Crest Farm Bed & Breakfast
Cuttingsville

Mountain View Creamery
East Burke

Rose Apple Acres Farm
North Troy

The Inn at Shelburne Farms
Shelburne

West Mountain Inn
Arlington

Broadview Farm Bed & Breakfast

Most farms don't qualify for a spot on the National Historic Register. After all, a building makes it onto the prestigious list if (1) someone famous owned it or slept there; (2) the building is particularly old, even for the area; or (3) its architecture is unusual for the area.

Broadview Farm made the list for the last reason. Molly Newell, who runs this farm with her husband, Joe, learned that her grandfather bought the place in 1904. But a traditional farmhouse didn't suit him—he came from Newport, Rhode Island—so he added lots of Italianate arches, which are common to his native area. Then it felt more like home.

Molly's grandfather ran it as a gentleman's farm, as did her parents, who bought the farm in 1957. Today, Molly and Joe are following the tradition on their 309-acre homestead, concentrating on maple sugaring and selling Christmas trees and wreaths. In fact, the bed and breakfast is open only from July through October, and in January and February—when there are lulls in the Newells' other businesses. These other businesses are of considerable size: the sugar grove has almost two thousand taps, which Joe wants to make thirty-five hundred. "We already have requests for more syrup than we make," he says, which is up to four hundred gallons a year. The farm's medium amber syrup was selected as the best in the state in 1992, and each guest gets a small jug of syrup to take home.

Then there are the twenty-five hundred Christmas trees planted in the field in front of the house, which take an average of ten years to grow to adequate living-room size.

Joe also keeps a couple of oxen, which he uses to haul a sleigh filled with neighborhood children in winter up the hill to the sugarhouse, along with a goat to keep the oxen company.

The road that passes in front of the main house served as the Boston Post Road in the nineteenth century. The house, which was built in the early 1800s, was a stagecoach inn on the route. Today, in winter, a trail on the network of the Vermont Association of Snow Travelers passes right by the house, and the constant buzzing of snowmobiles enlivens the silent cold six months of a Vermont winter.

The four guest rooms upstairs are filled with the artifacts of the lives of Molly's relatives. In what she calls the children's room, there's a picture of her father and his twin sister as children in front of the farmhouse. A pair of Molly's aunt's shoes hang above the bureau. In the Whittier room, named for her opera singer aunt, Harriet Whittier, a pair of old pointe shoes and old silver brushes and combs rest on the table.

There are also lots of old photographs of the sugaring operation at the farm that hang throughout the house. "I find fascinating things, so I put them all out," says Molly.

For company at the farm, guests can visit with a golden retriever named Cooper and a cat named Florence. Ask Joe for a tour of the sugarhouse; he'll happily oblige. He retired from the army in 1986, when he and Molly moved to Broadview. "We're doing exactly what we set out to do," says Molly.

Joe's guided tours of the sugarhouse have an ulterior motive, whether he's leading guests or some of the neighborhood schoolchildren. "If even one person is interested in the business," he says, "then they'll replace me when I'm finished."

In addition to the Christmas trees and sugar taps, Joe also cuts almost fifty cords of wood a year to heat the house and to boil down sap. So if you're interested in "the business," I wouldn't hold my breath—it looks as though he's going to be around for a while.

Molly and Joe Newell
Broadview Farm Bed & Breakfast
RFD 2, Box 153
St. Johnsbury, VT 05819
802-748-9902
$
Children welcome
Open July through October and January through February

Harvey's Mountain View Inn & Farm

Harvey's is a real Vermont tradition. Don and Maggie Harvey opened their house to guests in 1960 and never looked back. Maggie is a third-generation Vermonter. The first in her line—her grandfather—was the Vermonter who sold the von Trapps the land for Trapp Family Lodge up in Stowe.

Don's a sixth-generation Vermonter. In 1810 his great-great-great-grandfather started farming where the inn now stands; his great-grandson began farming at what is known as the home farm, down at the T in the road, just before you get to Harvey's. He also started taking in guests at the beginning of this century in that house, so farming and taking in guests seem to be in the Harvey blood.

Today, the home farm serves as the base for guests who want to help out with farm chores or just observe. The farm consists of six hundred

Holstein cow and calf

acres. The Harveys who live there today have 110 Holsteins—half of which are milkers—and they also grow hay, alfalfa, and corn.

"But," says Maggie, "there's not much that guests can help with as it's all so automated. They can watch the milking and go down to the older barn and watch the calves. In fact, children like to feed the calves."

Which brings us to the most important thing about Harvey's: families are very welcome here, as are couples. In fact, there's more for children to do than for their parents. They can pet the horses, go swimming, ride a pony, fish in the pond, and feed the geese, ducks, and rabbits. If one of the small fry catches a small fry, Maggie will cook it for the family for breakfast.

"They're never in their parents' hair because there's too much for them to do," says Maggie about her younger guests. She adds that the peace and quiet of the farm helps put life in perspective. As such, the farm has saved more than a few marriages; it's been recommended by several ministers as a getaway for couples who are having a hard time.

In addition to the farm activities, the Harveys offer hayrides at sunset for the whole family, followed by a marshmallow roast. Both dinner and breakfast are served at the inn; the food tends toward the type your grandmother would make when you visited her: chicken a la king, hot fresh bread with lots of butter, and spice cake with thick frosting, and for breakfast, fluffy pancakes served with plenty of bacon.

The rooms are comfortable with utilitarian furnishings that can withstand a summer's worth of small children on vacation. Many of the families that stay here come back the same week year after year. Children forge friendships that are renewed each year, and parents can catch up with each other, too.

The Harveys also rent out a small two-bedroom chalet by the week for guests who want a little more privacy as well as the option of preparing their own meals.

Maggie and Don Harvey
Harvey's Mountain View Inn & Farm
Rochester, VT 05767
802-767-4273
$$ MAP
Children welcome
Open year-round

Hill Farm Inn

After two and a half years of searching for the perfect inn, Regan and John Chichester finally found the Hill Farm Inn in Arlington, and in February 1993 they began in earnest to make guests comfortable in the thirteen-room inn.

But winter in Vermont is rarely benevolent, especially on brand-new innkeepers, so a few weeks later when the Blizzard of '93 hit Hill Farm, it was particularly wrathful and blew the tractor barn off its foundation. Other innkeepers might have thought, Uh-oh, did we do the right thing? But John put the barn back on the foundation and went about the business of running an inn on historic farmland as if nothing had happened.

Though John and Regan's plans for the inn include having fifty beefalo grazing on their sixty-acre homestead from May through October, Hill Farm got its start as a dairy farm. In fact, guests can still see the old silo foundations, and the old dairy barn is still standing. It's a big barn, and guests can go inside with John if they're curious, though it seems a bit haunted: the moos of the ghosts of hundreds of cows seem to resonate off the batten board walls. In a small room in the tractor barn, meant for guests to park their bicycles, they will see old calendars, receipts, and phone numbers. Check out the old snow roller that John says has been there forever.

It's a little spooky, all these signs of an earlier hustle and bustle, but the Vermont Central Railroad still runs right by the house, and its whistle can be heard several times a week.

In the main house, built in 1830, a spinning wheel sits in the hallway on the second floor. In a closet upstairs, there's part of an original wall painting that dates back to the early days of the house. Back then, an artist would paint a sample of his work in a closet for the owner's approval before proceeding to the hallway.

A large sitting room in the main house contains couches, lots of books, and a piano. The dining room has oak tables with fresh flowers on each. Classical music from a local public radio station plays in the house all day.

The other guest house was built in 1790 and has a rare—for Vermont—slate roof. There's a woodstove in the entryway and a sitting area with a brick hearth. You can still see the original beams, so you know you're in a house that's more than two centuries old. In mid-May, as you walk through the gardens between the two houses, the French lilac bushes scent the air with a heady perfume.

At 6:30 every night except Wednesdays, Regan serves up a four-course dinner for guests by request. A sample menu is spicy tomato soup, salad, chicken breasts with pecan sauce, rice, vegetables, and apple crisp and ice cream for dessert. Afterward, you can sit outside on the porch and watch the sun as it sets over the Green Mountains.

Neither John nor Regan had worked in an inn before Hill Farm; Regan worked as a textile designer, and John spent fourteen years working at Christie's Auction House in New York, which explains the period decorations and furnishings in each individually decorated guest room. But they'd visited many inns, and through the process they learned what they wanted in an inn of their own.

Hill Farm is the result.

Regan and John Chichester
Hill Farm Inn
RR 2, Box 2015
Arlington, VT 05250
802-375-2269 or 800-882-2545
$$, dinner optional
Children welcome
Open year-round

Hivue Bed & Breakfast

At Hivue Bed & Breakfast, the one vivid memory you will take with you is of the stomper dolls.

But before we get to that, the farm part of Hivue is a seventy-six-acre primitive tree farm that consists of black walnut trees, white pine, ash, birch, and black cherry. A primitive tree farm is basically an upgraded forest in a conservation area with definite restrictions placed on development. Wini and Bill Reuschle, hosts at Hivue, put in an interpretive nature trail through the woods and fields. The written trail guide, put together with the help of the local division of the Vermont Department of Forests, Parks and Recreation, points out the types of trees and rocks in the forest, and helps the walker to identify sites where glacier activity was heaviest, as well as an old sheep fence, and holes in trees that were created by woodpeckers.

On the screened back porch on the second floor of the house, guests can see where the trail cuts through the gently sloping hill. Look for the plastic Halloween pumpkin that Wini uses as a landmark. The bird books in the bookshelf will help you identify some of the many birds that fly through the wildlife habitat, and the beaver-gnawed logs on top of the bookcase will give you some idea of the degree of beaver activity in the brook on the property.

You can see two horses—Pico and Missy—graze in the pasture. Tina, an eighteen-year-old silky terrier, and Patchy, a mutt, will keep you company on the porch.

Okay, now to the stomper dolls. At breakfast, Bill, Wini, and Wini's brother, Larry, all sit down to eat with the guests.

About ten minutes into the meal, Bill asks, "Wini, can I tell some jokes?" Wini, a great straight (wo)man, replies, "Ask the guests."

What a setup. Of course we agree, and Bill proceeds to tell many of the clean, corny jokes a favorite uncle used to tell in the sixties. After they run their course—and Larry tells a few of his own—we all turn back to the meal.

Ten minutes later, Bill clears his throat again. "Wini, can I entertain?" Wini, again, says, "Ask the guests."

Bill pushes his chair away from the head of the table, almost into the living room. He opens a suitcase that just happens to be nearby and takes out a long, thin plank of wood. Then he sits on it. He puts a tape into a portable tape recorder and presses the button. It's "Lawrence Welk Plays America's Best-Loved Songs," complete with accordion. Bill reaches into the suitcase and pulls out what looks like a wooden marionette with a long stick in its back. He holds the stick so that the doll stands forward on the plank while his other hand taps on the board, in steady rhythm to Welk's everpresent accordion strains. Thus we are treated to a twenty-minute performance of stomper dolls painted to look like everything from Santa Claus to a horse.

Pancakes grow cold while we look on the scene with bemusement. After the performance, Bill hands each guest an oval piece of wood with two holes in it, which he calls his version of a worry stone.

Don't expect country inn–type furnishings if you visit Hivue. The decor at the farm belies its Vermont location. Decorated in a more utilitarian way than at other farms described in this book, the four guest rooms and the common space tend toward modern suburbia, perhaps all the more to serve as an incongruous backdrop for Bill's stomper dolls.

The bed at Hivue was comfortable, and the food was good, but the main thing I remember about Hivue are those dolls. As Bill says, "The reason for the stomper dolls is that people stay in so many different places that they seem to blend together after a while. With us, they remember the stomper dolls."

In fact, not too long ago, Bill and Wini were at a conference with a couple from San Diego. When the Reuschles mentioned that they ran a B&B in Vermont, the couple from California said they know a couple who stayed at a B&B in Vermont, and the man had stomper dolls.

Nuff said.

Wini and Bill Reuschle
Hivue Bed & Breakfast
RR 1, Box 1023
Brandon, VT 05733-9704
802-247-3042
$$
Children welcome
Open year-round

Homeplace

You're going to have to travel quite a distance to get to Homeplace because you sure won't stumble across it. But once you get here, you probably won't want to venture out again. This remote farm B&B is a quiet haven for people who want to soak up the atmosphere of a small working farm.

Mariot Huessy designed the house, which sits on 110 acres, in 1969 to fit the eleven children that she and her husband, Hans, a retired professor at the University of Vermont Medical School, raised between them. And yes, they all grew up here.

Mariot started the B&B in 1985 when the last child left, and two people rattling around such a huge house seemed indulgent. But all the children come back for big, boisterous reunions, which, more often than not, could be the reason for the no vacancy that Mariot might have told you about when you called.

Of course they accept children and families, who are welcome to help with some of the chores for the horses, sheep, chickens, ducks, dogs, and cats that populate the farm. The Huessys raise all their own produce and meat; Mariot cultivates the flowers while Hans tends the vegetable garden. There's a swing set in the backyard, along with a pond with floats and docks and walking paths all around. You reach the pond via a series of fenced-in gardens; just remember to close the gate after you so the sheep don't get loose.

Mariot says that 75 percent of the people who visit Homeplace come because of the animals and the gardens. "And people come here for the quiet," says Mariot. "They also go biking and hiking, and we get a lot of retired professors from UVM who stay here. Because we're way off the main drag, it eliminates the people who usually stay in hotels and motels." Most guests come in summer, though in winter guests have the advantage of lingering in the huge living room with a stone floor and several seating areas. Sit on the sofa that faces the fireplace; you can either read for hours

Face to face with a farm cat

or stare into the flames. Nothing short of sleep or breakfast will make you want to move.

Most of the furniture in the house is from Germany, where Hans grew up. Since old German houses don't have closets, there are big armoires all through Homeplace, along with china cabinets, dark Germanic furniture, and a music area with an old piano, recorders, violins, and a guitar. The influence of a large family is everywhere you look.

The unusual six-sided barn is quite musical, between the bleats of the sheep and the bells that hang from their necks. The farm literally surrounds the house.

Breakfast consisted of fresh fruit and pancakes that were more like crepes, to the delight of the couple from Quebec who were visiting during my stay.

At Homeplace, you think you'll catch everything the first time through, from the stained glass window in the entrance to the iron cat doorstop in your room. But the second and third time you pass through a room or garden at Homeplace, you'll always see something new.

Mariot and Hans Huessy
Homeplace
RR 2, Box 367
Jericho, VT 05465
802-899-4694
$$
Children welcome
Open year-round

Hound's Folly

Though the farm is called Hound's Folly and it's in the town of Mount Holly, the main draw here is sheep, an average of more than a hundred most of the year. There are three dogs—two border collies named Ben and Chip, and Max, a fourteen-year-old dachshund—and plenty of dog figurines, wall hangings, and other canine decorations all through the house. Nevertheless, the major attraction at this twenty-acre farm run by sisters Elise and Luise Durr is sheep, which guests seem to enjoy.

"Sheep serve as icebreakers with our guests," says Elise, who moved to Vermont with her sister in 1978. "Guests ask a lot of questions, like if they bite, and what do they eat? Some guests want to take sheep back home with them, and others already have sheep at home. We have a friend with goats who says sheep people are the salt of the earth while goat people are just plain weird. But this part of Vermont is cow country, so I don't know what *that* means."

What it means is that many guests initially wander out into the pasture to watch the sheep skitter away—sheep are shy animals—and then decide they'll do something to make the sheep like them, which includes hauling water and grain, and in spring, helping with lambing. Many guests choose to stay put, however. "We don't ask guests to do any chores," says Luise. "They just offer." One man from New York helped stack a few cords of wood. "He just couldn't sit still," Luise remembers.

Children particularly enjoy giving bottles to the lambs in spring, and in winter they can feed fruits and vegetables to the sheep. But sheep are sheep and children are children, which means that when a sheep sees a small child, it runs, and the child chases the sheep, which makes it worse. The sheep never give up; it's the child who usually grows tired of the fruitless chase.

The Durrs bought the house in 1978 and spent five years fixing it up. They opened the bed and breakfast in 1984 and got their first three sheep that same year, initially to keep the pasture mowed. "Lots of people around here have a couple of sheep to keep the pasture down, then they end up in the freezer," says Elise. "But we name all of them, and we have so many because Luise hates to get rid of them," though they do keep about twenty lambs for their regular meat customers.

The three guest rooms are quite comfortable and large, and the shared bath in the 1810 Colonial house has a clawfoot tub and a sheepskin rug. Downstairs, there are two sitting areas, and a family room with a big woodstove and a TV and VCR.

Unlike most farm B&Bs in New England, Hound's Folly is busier in winter, because it is just eight miles from the Okemo ski area. For many downhill skiers, who prefer to stay slopeside, eight miles might as well be eight hundred. Hound's Folly is for the adventurous skier who doesn't particularly care for the apres-ski scene.

Elise and Luise Durr
Hound's Folly
Box 591
Mount Holly, VT 05758
802-259-2718
$$
Children welcome
Open year-round

Knoll Farm Country Inn

Knoll Farm looks much the way a small sustenance farm in Vermont looked back in the early 1800s. The accommodations and meals fit the bill as well.

Knoll Farm's owner, Ann Day, focuses on serving three farm-grown, home-cooked meals a day, while offering comfortable beds—many are family heirlooms—and a chance for guests to do as much or as little as they like.

There's nothing fancy at the 150-acre Knoll Farm, which may be why guests find it so easy to relax so quickly. The guest rooms are like grandma's, with throw rugs, dark, heavy dressers from the turn of the century, and quilts and coverlets to match. Each of the farm's four bedrooms has two beds; Room #1 has the kind of bed I've always loved, the kind you have to climb up into. It's a massive mahogany four-poster with palm fronds deeply carved into the posters and headboard. Ann says it came from Hawaii.

Outside, the old bank barn has three levels. The first floor is home to the farm's animals, the second floor is for hay and storage, and the third floor contains various old carriages from horse-and-buggy days: one has a lantern and another served as a hearse.

Down on the first floor, many of the horses are twenty years old and more; Ann calls it her Home for Old Retired Horses. A stall on the far wall contains a pig, and another holds two cats. It's a bit strange to look into an animal stall and see a couple of cats—Christine and TC—curled up into a ball. But these cats are constantly at odds with Ann's cat, so at night they're relegated to their own stall. Which is fine in summer, because most of the farm's other animals are in the pasture.

In addition to the horses, Ann raises Scottish Highland cattle, and a few sheep and chickens. There's also a large organic vegetable garden, flower and herb gardens, and an apple orchard as well. Guests frequently

Scottish Highland cattle at Knoll Farm

help out with gardening, haying, cutting wood, and feeding and brushing the horses.

A small pond is located down a knoll from the farmhouse, with majestic views of the mountains. In front of the house, the Adirondack chairs and hammock offer another vantage point.

Knoll Farm serves as a microcosm of the history of agriculture in Vermont. Still being farmed, it has been nominated for the National Register of Historic Sites. Not much has changed since the land was first farmed in 1803, when it began as a sheep farm, then progressed to dairy farming and maple sugaring by the eve of the Civil War. Then, at the height of the Depression, farming ceased to be the principal activity. In fact, Knoll Farm then followed the pattern of land usage in the Mad River Valley of Vermont as, by necessity, residents switched their allegiance from farming to tourism. But unlike the gift shops and restaurants in the valley a mile down the road, Knoll Farm has maintained the integrity of the land through the pastures and farm buildings.

At meals, there's plenty of food—dinner consists of five courses— and the meals are heavy on vegetables and light on meat.

The farm is open from May through the end of October. Ann plans many specialized weekend and week-long seminars in Spanish, nature, and women's career options throughout the summer. The inn reopens for the winter season just after Christmas until March, and is right down the road from the Mad River Glen and Sugarbush ski areas. There's also ample cross-country ski opportunities on the farm and at nearby centers.

Ann Day
Knoll Farm Country Inn
Bragg Hill Road
Waitsfield, VT 05673
802-496-3939
$$ AP
Children over 8 welcome
Open May through October and late December through March

Lake Ledge Farm

Lake Ledge is about as far west in Vermont as you can get, tucked as it is on the shores of Lake Champlain. It's quiet, removed from major highways, and a few miles from the historic Mount Independence site, which directly faces Fort Ticonderoga across the lake in New York State. Linda and Charlie Peake enjoy having families visit Lake Ledge. Linda says that children are the key for the entire family's vacation.

"Children will come in the house or run out into the pasture and feel comfortable right away," says Linda. "Then, the parents are able to relax." They do so by sitting on the porch or in the hammock under the grape arbor, or walking down the gentle grassy slope to the lake and just drinking in the beauty of the view.

The Peakes keep forty sheep and a dozen chickens. A couple of lambs graze freely in front of the porch. Though Lake Ledge shares the road with several other larger farms, this farm is an authentic throwback to the days before the automated farming of their neighbors, down to the old bell outside that used to be tolled to let the workers know when it was mealtime. Today, Linda rings it to alert guests out in the field of long-distance phone calls.

The Peakes moved to Vermont from New Jersey in 1987 specifically to operate a farm that takes in guests. Linda says that they're used to having people live in their house because she previously rented out rooms to college students.

Inside the farmhouse, which dates from the early 1800s, the breakfast room has an old baby grand piano, a fireplace with a separate bake oven built right next to it, and a refrigerator for guests to use. There's another sitting room toward the back of the house with a wonderful view of the lake. Upstairs, three guest rooms share the hall bathroom, though two have half-baths of their own. These bedrooms look out onto the lake. In one, a large braided rug covers the floor, and quilts and crocheted throws are on the pencil-post queen-sized and twin beds; an antique blanket chest sits at the foot of the queen-sized bed. The other back bedroom contains a white iron double bed and a smaller twin.

Linda refers to the third guest room as the Rooster Room. Located in the front of the house, it's closest to the henhouse and has a double bed and a twin, which belonged to her grandmother. Fresh flowers and plants

Your children will make new friends on a farm

are in all the rooms, and if Linda knows that children are coming, she'll put out books that are appropriate for their age. She worked as a preschool director in New Jersey, and today teaches at a nearby school in addition to running the farm and B&B.

When you arrive at Lake Ledge, you'll be greeted by the canine welcoming committee with a membership of one. Buster, a mutt with some German shepherd in him, is a typical friendly farm dog who follows guests on their various excursions around the farm, whether they're kite flying, fishing, playing croquet or volleyball, or bird-watching. Linda says that owls, blue heron, chimney swifts, and bald eagles regularly fly over the farm. There are three marinas nearby where guests can rent canoes and paddleboats.

There's also a public town cemetery on the land, which you'll pass on the right just before you get to the house. Buster gladly accompanies guests as they examine the inscriptions, which date from the early nineteenth century. Or you can just relax on the porch with Linda and Charlie and look at the gently rolling hills, the fluffy sheep, and the small cemetery with bleached stones that perch atop the hill just like a white picket fence.

Linda and Charlie Peake
Lake Ledge Farm
RR 1, Box 70
Orwell, VT 05760
802-948-2347
$$
Children welcome
Open year-round

Lareau Farm Country Inn

Dan and Sue Easley, who've run Lareau Farm Country Inn since 1984, like to tell guests about the time their chickens were kidnapped. "Friends who worked as hiking guides were visiting us—they lived two miles up the hill. We had just gotten a new flock of chickens, and after our friends left, we couldn't find the chickens.

"Not long after they left, we got a phone call from them, saying that our chickens were running around their yard. 'Impossible,' I said, but since we couldn't find them anywhere, we drove up and there they were. We good-naturedly accused our friends of chicken-napping, and caught the birds and brought them back home.

"The next time they visited, the same thing happened. We went back up to rescue them, and figured out that while our friends' truck was parked in our yard, the chickens thought their wheel springs would be a good place to roost. And so they did. We never did figure out how the chickens put up with the ride, but the next time our friends came to visit, we looked under the truck before they left."

Chickens escape, the Easleys' four dogs get Christmas cards from guests, and children who visit make drawings of the sleigh horses—Holly, Dolly, and Molly—and hang them up in the barn. That's the kind of place Lareau Farm is—laid-back and comfortable. Nothing ever seems to fluster Dan and Sue; after all, nine years in the inn and farm business is a long time.

Guests regularly wander from one lazy-day activity to another. Ask Dan where the old bridge abutment is; it used to be a covered bridge and part of old Route 100 that crossed the river. Today, there's a knoll above the swimming hole in the river with a rope that hangs from a tree that you can use to swing into the water.

Many families come for the four horses, four dogs, three cats, assorted chickens—when they're around—and sleigh rides in winter, as well as to be close to Sugarbush, which is just down the road. Guests can poke through the barn, walk through the sixty-seven acres of meadows and woods, admire the unusual flower and vegetable gardens—some with raised circular beds—or just take the dogs for a walk. Families are welcome here. One part of the inn has double and single rooms side by side for parents and their children. Of course, the favorite activity for some guests is to sit in a rocker on the porch at the back of the house and watch the grass grow. There's even a restaurant on the premises that serves flat-bread, which is like pizza but without the sauce. Breakfast is traditional country, such as fresh fruit and French toast with Vermont maple syrup.

The inn has thirteen rooms in all, and has been run as an inn of sorts since 1955, when Florette Lareau took in boarders when the family stopped dairy farming after twenty years. Before that, a Doctor Stoddard, who served as a physician in the revolutionary war with General Waits-field, homesteaded on his four hundred acres of land, which was in the same family until the Lareaus took it over in 1936. The Easleys are currently designing a historical walking path through their land that tells the history of its use, and it will pass a wooded area where Doctor Stoddard and his wife are buried.

Susan and Dan Easley
Lareau Farm Country Inn
Box 563, Route 100
Waitsfield, VT 05673
802-496-4949 or 800-833-0766
$$ includes breakfast, other meals optional
Children welcome
Open year-round

Liberty Hill Farm

The first thing you'll notice about Liberty Hill Farm, located right off Route 100, are the smells. When you first step out of your car, you'll be greeted by the ubiquitous sign of a dairy farm: the odor of manure. When you enter the house, you'll find the welcoming aroma of freshly baked something or other, and you'll delight in anticipation of what is to be that night's dinner.

That host Beth Kennett prepares everything from scratch is indicative of the farm as a whole: Liberty Hill is a thriving, old-fashioned dairy farm that many people visit because of its perceived museumlike quality.

The Kennetts started taking in people in 1986 when the price of milk plummeted. To keep the tradition of dairy farming going, they decided to open their home to guests.

In addition to all the smells, the farm is also a veritable cacophony of sounds: roosters serve as alarm clocks, tractors putt-putt their way past the house, cows moo, and the dog barks. But all these sounds conspire to provide guests with peaceful sleep, a better tonic than any sleeping pill. Chickens, ducks, turkeys, rabbits, assorted barn cats, and of course the Holsteins are never far away. They provide a gentle humming all day long that lulls you to sleep at night.

Then there's the food. You'll feel as though you're sitting down with the Waltons: casseroles, baskets, and pans filled with everything homemade are passed and repassed while tales of fishing, milking, and antiquing whirl around the breakfast and dinner table.

The farm is open year-round, and guests come for skiing, fishing, hiking, and canoeing, and to work in the barn. If you like to feed calves, pitch hay, and tell the cows to "gwan" when it's time to go out for the night, you can keep busy all day and night. Beth tells of some high-ranking corporate executives who've been known to get into their flannels and jeans and head for the barn at six each morning for a week, and to claim that they want to trade places with Bob.

Others watch wide-eyed as Bob nonchalantly milks the cows, shovels manure, and artificially inseminates the herd—the nod to modern dairy farming given at Liberty Hill along with the milking machines, whose rhythm brings to mind the snare-drum button on the Magnus portable organs popular in the 1970s. The barn cats keep time on the rafters, performing a half-crazed conga caused by the smell of fresh milk that's just beyond paw's reach.

Liberty Hill is right in the middle of ski country, halfway between Killington and Sugarbush. It is unusual among farms that take in guests because Beth also serves dinner. "When we started there were no restaurants nearby for guests," says Beth, "so if we wanted them to stay, we had to offer them dinner." In fact, mealtime is a significant part of what makes Liberty Hill special, because the Kennetts eat dinner with guests.

"Our whole house is shared," she adds. "Once in a while, that's not what someone's looking for, but most people quickly adapt."

Beth and Bob Kennett
Liberty Hill Farm
Rochester, VT 05767
802-767-3926
$$ MAP
Children welcome
Open year-round

Maple Crest Farm Bed & Breakfast

"We're not Old McDonald's Farm, and we're not a petting zoo," says Donna Smith, innkeeper at Maple Crest Farm. Instead, the B&B, decorated in the Victorian style, is more like the house of an elegant grandmother. Maple Crest followed the trend of dairy farming in Vermont and discontinued the dairying some time ago. The focus today is on maple syrup and selling hay from the 330-acre homestead, which has been in the Smith family for six generations. The farm still has forty head of Hereford beef cattle as well as a couple of pigs, but the cows are out in the far pastures from May through November, so there's not a whole lot of farm activity for guests to see.

Instead, many of the people who come to Maple Crest are recently retired and traveling, or young couples who need a breather from the city. Maple Crest is a wonderful place for them to do it, with six bed-and-breakfast rooms. The twenty-seven-room Federal-style house was built in 1808 as a tavern and stagecoach stop to serve travelers on the old Crown Point Road. In fact, the guest room right off the hall to the left was the original tavern room and, as such, is one of the few rooms in the house with floors that are not original. Thousands of pairs of boots from travelers of almost two hundred years ago wore away the floorboards, which had to be replaced.

Curio cabinets are throughout the house, each with glassware, knickknacks, and figurines that take up every available inch of the shelves. In the parlor sitting room downstairs, an old upright piano stands against one wall, flanked by a Victrola. Donna regularly holds quilt workshops here, and church and other small-group retreats meet here also. In the adjacent common room, there's a TV with many sofas and comfortable chairs. In winter, a low fire is always going; the wing chair by the fireplace is a hot commodity when the mercury plummets.

Maple Crest also has two apartments available for guests; each has two bedrooms, a kitchenette, private bath, and living room and can fit five people comfortably. Period furniture, rocking chairs, and lots of new and old books adorn the rooms. One apartment even has an outside deck. Donna encourages families to stay in the apartments for the space and freedom they afford children.

If guests really want to assist on the farm, they can help collect sap buckets in spring, and watch the Smiths boil down the sap to make syrup. Donna looks at the farm as a retreat for guests instead of a place to exert yourself: "It's a place to relax, hike, and love the land, and then go back to the city rejuvenated."

Breakfast at Maple Crest of course features the farm's own maple syrup; buttermilk pancakes, homemade muffins and jams, and fresh fruit are always available. Guests often take some of Maple Crest's syrup home with them. Instead of buying fancy grade syrup, be adventurous and try either the medium amber or medium dark amber grade, which provide a stronger, heartier maple flavor that will remind you of Maple Crest when you get back home.

Donna and Bill Smith
Maple Crest Farm Bed & Breakfast
Box 120
Cuttingsville, VT 05738
802-492-3367
Children welcome
$$
Open year-round

Mountain View Creamery

The Mountain View Creamery is magical, a rare treasure with 440 intact, quiet acres that urge you to explore them.

The farm was purchased in 1883 by local benefactor Elmer A. Darling, who was largely responsible for the economic success of tiny East Burke. By the time Darling had finished his land acquisitions, he had the largest farm in Vermont, with 953 acres. He was part owner of the elegant Fifth Avenue Hotel in Manhattan, and most of the food produced on the farm was shipped to the hotel; this included six hundred pounds of butter a month and sixty pounds of cheese each day.

The stately brick main house, which served as the creamery, has seven bed-and-breakfast rooms named after local towns: Sutton, Sheffield, and Wheelock are three. There's an understated, casual elegance to the inn that owner Marilyn Pastore has worked hard to attain. There are several sitting rooms downstairs, an ice chest in the lobby, and braided rugs on every floor, which are painted cement. The breakfast room still contains the old steam engine that provided the power to run the creamery machines; antique furnishings are found in the common areas and in each bedroom.

There are a number of restored farm buildings scattered across the land. The weathervane atop each building tells its purpose: the dairy barn has a cow weathervane that measures five feet in length; on top of the creamery is a butter churn. Behind the 1912 barn is an extensive perennial and vegetable garden; there are Adirondack chairs all around the property, and a swing hangs from an old oak.

Marilyn Pastore bought the farm in 1987 and today runs the bed and breakfast year-round while she slowly restores all the farm buildings to their previous grandeur. The Darling farm was a miniature community, with an icehouse, threshing barn, dairy barn, tool-sharpening shop, piggery, and even a building to wash and dry the Morgan workhorses. In recent years, it was used as a cross-country ski shed.

The clock on top of the 1912 post-and-beam barn chimes on the half-hour. The structure was a model for nineteenth-century agricultural efficiency. Upstairs, hay was stored. Farmhands would spread hay evenly throughout the barn, almost up to the rafters. When it was time to feed the horses, they'd rake the hay over to what looks like half-moon hot tub structures at the sides of the barn, lift up the covers, and let the hay drop. The horses were about sixteen hands high, and you can see where they chewed on the bottom of the windows of the barn.

The building to the right of the creamery has been converted to condominiums: take a look at them if you have time. The attention to detail is everywhere in this re-creation of a nineteenth-century gracious home with every modern amenity.

Though in Elmer Darling's day there were one hundred Jerseys roaming the pastures, today there are three Herefords and one Holstein, which Marilyn and her husband keep as pets. The Boston & Maine Railroad still passes by the farm, evident from a distant whistle that you can hear best if you're wandering around the farm, which could take all day. Roxy, Marilyn's terrier, might follow you around.

Marilyn is not sure what she wants to do with the entire farm—a scaled-down version of northwest Vermont's Shelburne Museum is a possibility—but in the meantime she works to slowly renovate farm buildings and operate the bed and breakfast.

The wind comes up through the trees, the train whistles, and as you wander around the farm, you might be aware of Elmer Darling's ghost following you.

Marilyn Pastore
Mountain View Creamery
Box 355
East Burke, VT 05832
802-626-9924
$$
Children over 12 welcome
Open year-round

Rose Apple Acres Farm

Rose Apple Acres Farm is just under a mile from the Canadian border as the crow flies—three miles if by car—and many people come to stay as a stop between Boston and Montreal.

But this is to underestimate the real gold of the fifty-two-acre farm: even Cam Mead, who's owned the bed and breakfast with her husband, Jay, since 1986, says she thinks the farm is relaxing and very quiet. It's quiet all day and night, she says, except for the birds, the bleating of the sheep, the occasional bee, and the wind chimes on the porch.

Some people, when they travel, want to have a lot of choices available to them, but in this corner of the state you have to leave that behind. The best choice to make on a sunny, breezy summer morning at Rose Apple Acres is to sit on the porch and read or nap, walk through the fields to the pond, or wander through the barn, where Cam's son, Courtney, keeps sheep, goats, Belgian horses, and Jersey cattle. The barn is an unusual long one, with plenty of room for the animals and the sleighs and wagons that are stored there.

The Meads raise much of what they eat, with enough left over to sell. In addition to making apple cider and wine from their orchard, the gardens produce broccoli, corn, cauliflower, tomatoes, pumpkins, and peas, and they make their own sauerkraut. There are also a number of other farms on East Hill Road, where Rose Apple Acres is located.

The end of the Long Trail, which runs the length of Vermont, is in North Troy, and Cam will transport or pick up hikers from the trailhead. In winter, guests can go downhill skiing at nearby Jay Peak or go cross-country skiing or snowshoeing through the pastures.

But most of all, people come to the farm to relax, because it's secluded; Cam suggests it's best for guests to stay two or three nights to get a feel for the area, no matter the season.

There are three guest rooms at Rose Apple Acres; the room I stayed in upstairs, which had a private bath, reminded me of my bedroom when

Belgians at Rose Apple Acres

I was growing up, with maple dressers and paneled walls. But there was one big difference: this room had a great view of the mountains, and at night the silence was so profound that it almost seemed loud.

The farm looks out onto the Canadian Sutton Range on one side, and Jay Peak on the other. The faraway blinking lights to the northeast of the house are in the Quebec town of Mansonville. The house was built at the turn of the century, and at one time drew a crowd from both sides of the border on warm Sunday afternoons, when the Augers, a family of local circus high-wire walkers, performed at the farm.

"People used to line up on the road and watch the Augers walk on a wire a hundred feet off the ground without a net," says Cam. "Today, I feel that the house gets real excited when an Auger comes to visit."

If you're not an Auger, at least the farm's two dogs, Molly the collie or Jimmy, an Afghan hound, will get excited at your arrival. In fact, you might have trouble getting rid of Jimmy, whom the Meads have dubbed "The Velcro Dog."

"He just sticks to you," says Jay.

Cam and Jay Mead
Rose Apple Acres Farm
RR 2, Box 300
East Hill Road
North Troy, VT 05859
802-988-4300
$
Children welcome
Open year-round

The Inn at Shelburne Farms

The first thing you must know about the Inn at Shelburne Farms is that it is not your typical farm—or inn, for that matter.

The inn and farm were first built in 1887 by a Vanderbilt couple as a combination experimental farm and summer retreat. With 110 rooms, admittedly it's not your typical country house. In fact, it looks more like a castle.

Today, the Queen Anne–style home contains twenty-four bedrooms for guests—seventeen with private baths—all with original furnishings. In one, the Yellow Room, a clawfoot tub sits in a bathroom that's bigger than most bedrooms. The two twin beds in one large room seem almost like cradles, with large headboards and sideboards that envelop the mattresses. An old-fashioned armoire, a full-length standing mirror, and a fireplace complete the room, along with original lighting fixtures indicative of the style: a table lamp is a large fish that holds the bulb aloft. Freshly cut flowers from the gardens on Lake Champlain are found in each of the guest rooms.

The inn is open only from late spring through early fall because the central heating system was taken out during World War II to donate the scrap metal to the war effort. Lila Vanderbilt Webb extensively remodeled the house in 1899 in order to accommodate their many friends and guests with a staff of thirty.

This entertainment in the grand style started to lose its luster around 1915, when both the tax laws and the economy began to change. The Webbs began to sell off the land, and what started out as thirty-eight hundred acres today is just one thousand. The property slowly declined through the years, though it was still used as a summer house. In 1987 the Webb heirs decided to turn it into an inn.

This is a farm vacation in the grand style. It's easy to pretend you're the baron or baroness of Shelburne Farms. Sit on one of the brocaded chairs at the bay window that overlooks the lake, in the library amidst more than six thousand books—most of them belonged to Lila Vanderbilt Webb. Adjust your white gloves, tip your hat, and pretend you're overseeing your grounds that look out on the lake and to the Adirondacks in the distance.

Then proceed to the third floor, decorated more simply than the rest, since it was originally intended for visiting children and their nannies, and walk through the playroom, with antique blocks, books, and six-foot-high dollhouses.

Next, it's on to the formal dining room, where elegant breakfasts and dinners are served. Rack of lamb with rosemary sauce and eggs Shelburne—eggs Benedict with pancetta and fresh basil Hollandaise—are indicative of the fare.

Then it's out to the gardens, where lamb's ears, hollyhocks, and delphiniums bloom, along with a rose garden. To authentically re-create Lila's extensive gardens, landscape gardeners relied on her old garden books, seed catalogs, journals, and photographs for reference. A fountain with a lion's head empties into a lily pond, all with the backdrop of Lake Champlain.

On the rest of the farm you'll find walking trails, working dairy barns where you can watch Brown Swiss cows being milked and cheese being made, a children's farmyard, and an education center where programs at the nonprofit Shelburne Farms teach local children about the stewardship of agricultural and natural resources.

The Inn at Shelburne Farms
Shelburne, VT 05482
802-985-8498
$$$
Children welcome
Open from late spring through early fall

West Mountain Inn

It's a good thing that vacancies are usually quite limited at the West Mountain Inn in Arlington. If you had the chance to survey the thirteen guest rooms upstairs before you selected one, it might take a long time.

Quilts cover the canopy beds in the spacious, airy rooms, each with a unique character and named after a famous person with ties to Arlington. The Robert Frost room has rockers on the screened porch that overlooks the llama pasture. The Norman Rockwell room is an unusual, large treetop room on the third floor with a couple of beds with three curtained sleeping nooks. Other rooms have fireplaces and decks, and there's even a barrier-free room. In fact, the entire inn is handicap accessible.

The llamas keep company with a number of rabbits that wander around the land surrounding the inn. Some of the bunnies have one ear up and one ear down, the result of domestic rabbits mating with wild rabbits. In the barn, three llamas look at you dispassionately as you enter. Whistle, and their ears flatten. Come near them and they continue to stare. Basically, they're just not impressed.

No matter; there are lots of other things to catch your attention here. The inn's 150 acres have five miles of trails that meander through it, and if you'd like to make friends with a llama, a local guide leads hikers from the inn on a llama trek up the back of the mountain every Wednesday in summer and fall.

In the numerous sitting areas downstairs, you can play old pianos, find a collection of nutcrackers in one corner, and gaze into a big fish tank. In the game room, you can play chess and watch the birds gather at numerous bird feeders. Perhaps it should be called the wind chime room—it contains no fewer than sixteen.

The philosophy of Wes and Mary Ann Carlson, who bought the inn in 1978, is that everything ties together in nature, and they encourage guests to observe nature and be respectful of it. Guests can help feed the llamas in the morning. The Carlsons did keep birds inside at one time, but a guest pointed out that none of the other animals on the farm were caged, so why were the birds? Today, a huge empty bird cage graces the game room.

The inn started a vegetable and flower garden in 1993 because they had so much manure from the llamas that they didn't know what to do with it. The gardens now grow pumpkins, squash, beans, and other produce that the inn's dining room puts to good use.

The inn has published a cookbook with many recipes from the gourmet breakfasts and dinners. The Carlsons earmark the proceeds from the sale of the cookbook for a local scholarship fund for a student from Arlington High School.

Dinner is offered to guests and to the public, and features soup, salad, sorbet, and a number of heart-healthy entrees. Dessert and aromatic hazelnut coffee follow. Breakfast includes homemade granola, sour cream coffee cake, and the decidedly un-heart-healthy but delicious Ooey Gooey, featured in the West Mountain Inn cookbook.

Mary Ann and Wes Carlson
West Mountain Inn
Arlington, VT 05250
802-375-6516
$$$ MAP
Children welcome
Open year-round